INSPIRATIONS IN KILN-FORMED
GLASS

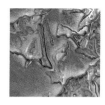

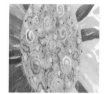

INSPIRATIONS IN KILN-FORMED

GLASS

25 PROJECTS FOR FUSING AND SLUMPING

GILLIAN HULSE

CONTENTS

First published in Great Britain
in 2009 by A&C Black Publishers Ltd
36 Soho Square, London W1D 3QY
www.acblack.com

Copyright © Breslich & Foss Ltd 2009
Text copyright © Gillian Hulse 2009

Photography: **Michael Wicks**
Design: **Elizabeth Healey**
Commissioning editor:
 Janet Ravenscroft
Project manager: **Kate Haxell**

This book was conceived and produced
by Breslich & Foss Ltd, London

A CIP catalogue record for this book is
available from the British Library

ISBN 978 1 408 11437 7

Printed and bound in China

10 9 8 7 6 5 4 3 2 1

INTRODUCTION

IN THE PAST FEW YEARS THE INTEREST IN GLASS has increased considerably due to the availability of reasonably priced glass kilns and the development of courses for all levels of ability. Glass is a fascinating material to work with, not only because of the beauty of its colour, texture and the way it reflects and refracts light, but also because it is such a versatile medium. If you were to visit an exhibition of work by glass artists you would discover a myriad of different styles and techniques, from large wall panels made using perhaps just two or three bands of colour, to complex abstract dishes incorporating pieces of copper and layers of frits.

This book is written for people who have had a little experience of making pieces of kiln-formed glass and who would like to explore further the techniques of fusing and slumping, the use of inclusions and ways of using fibre paper. In trying out some of the projects, I hope that you will find your own variations and make your own unique pieces.

GILLIAN HULSE

GETTING
STARTED

YOU DON'T NEED MUCH EQUIPMENT TO MAKE SIMPLE PIECES
OF KILN-FORMED GLASS. START WITH THE BASICS AND INVEST
IN MORE AS YOUR PASSION FOR GLASS DEVELOPS, AS IT
SURELY WILL. THIS CHAPTER DISCUSSES THE MATERIALS AND
TECHNIQUES YOU'LL NEED TO MAKE PROJECTS IN THIS BOOK.

WORKSHOP

ORGANISATION

If you are lucky enough to be able to design your workshop space then it is best to have a large table for cutting glass and assembling projects, a separate kiln area and plenty of deep shelving for storing glass and moulds. Light is another consideration, preferably natural daylight if possible.

However, most people have to work in whatever space is available and will need to make adaptations to suit the work they are doing.

HEALTH AND SAFETY

This is a topic that few people enjoy reading about but it is an essential aspect to working with glass and much of it is just commonsense.

GLASS

Think about what you are wearing: avoid open-toed shoes, loose clothes and tie your hair back if it is long.

An apron will protect your clothes from small shards of glass and dust.

The risk of cutting yourself can be minimised by storing glass safely in purpose-built racks, keeping your work space clean and clear of small pieces of glass, and using safe methods when cutting sheet glass.

Avoid eating and drinking in your work space and wear eye protection when cutting or grinding glass. When working with frits or powder, it is advisable to wear a respirator to prevent inhaling air-borne particles. It is worth installing an extractor fan if you are doing a lot of glass work.

FIBRE PAPER AND OTHER PRODUCTS

Fibre paper can be an irritant to skin and eyes and it may be best to wear gloves when using this material if you have sensitive skin. Fired fibre paper releases a dust that is dangerous to breathe and you should always wear

a respirator when working with it. Thinfire shelf paper turns to dust on firing and is easily removed by washing the glass in water.

Kilns and work surfaces can be cleaned using a vacuum cleaner with a High Efficiency Particulate filter. A respirator is necessary when you are mixing shelf primer as it contains silica, which can irritate airways; the same applies if you are scraping primer off kiln shelves.

KILNS

Your kiln needs to be sited in a place with plenty of ventilation (at least one metre/three feet from the wall) and on a non-flammable surface. Make sure that it is installed by a qualified electrician and that it has its own circuit. Ensure that flammable items are stored well away from the kiln and that you have a fire extinguisher in the work space – choose one suitable for all types of fire.

SAFETY EQUIPMENT
- Safety goggles
- Welder's glasses (if you ever need to look in the kiln while it is on)
- Respirator or dust mask
- Safety gloves for carrying large sheets of glass
- Latex or rubber gloves for use with chemicals
- First aid kit
- Fire extinguisher suitable for all types of fire

ABOVE *dust mask*

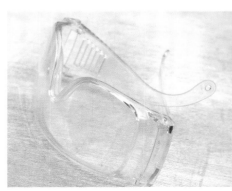

ABOVE *safety goggles*

TOOLS
AND MATERIALS

Listed here are the basic items you will need to make glass projects.

FOR CLEANING
- Glass cleaner.
- Vinegar – excellent for cleaning glass and leaves no residue.
- Isopropyl alcohol – good for removing pen marks from glass.
- Detergent – for cleaning glass after firing, remember to rinse glass in clear water afterwards.
- Lint-free paper towels.
- A sieve or plastic basket with holes – used for washing small pieces of glass.

FOR CUTTING
- Glass cutter – there are different cutters available and I prefer the type with an oil reservoir that feeds oil onto a high-quality cutting wheel. My preference is for the 'pistol grip' handle that provides a good grip when you are cutting glass (see below right).

ABOVE AND RIGHT *glass cutters*

- Glass cutter oil.
- Glass cutting surface, for example a Morton surface that catches all the small pieces of glass. You may also need a piece of board for cutting smaller pieces of glass on.
- Grozing pliers – these are used for breaking the glass after it is scored and for breaking off sharp edges. (It is sometimes useful to have two pairs of these pliers.)
- Circle cutter.
- Running pliers – for breaking glass that has not been cut sufficiently.
- Cutting square – for cutting straight lines.
- Steel rule.
- Fine, permanent marker pens in black and white – for drawing designs onto glass.
- Glass grinder – designed to grind and shape glass; some models can also be used with a drill attachment for drilling holes.

FOR ASSEMBLY

- Jewellery pliers – the round- or flat-nosed type are useful for working with small pieces of glass.
- Glues – glass glue for assembling work before firing; epoxy glue for assembling jewellery and putting together magnets and mirrors.
- Glue brush.
- Scribe – very useful for pushing small pieces of glass into position.
- Wire cutters.

KILNS AND KILN CONTROLLERS

The growing interest in working with glass has meant that there is now a bewildering array of different types of kiln available. It is not the purpose of this book to talk in great detail about what type of kiln you should choose, but the main things to bear in mind (apart, of course, from cost) are size and what sort of work you want to produce.

The smaller kilns are surprisingly inexpensive to run, but if you are thinking of buying a big kiln you will need to consider what kind of power supply you will need. It is worth contacting some of the kiln suppliers (see page 127) and finding out more about the various types of kiln that are on offer before making your decision. In my experience, the staff at these companies are very helpful and knowledgeable.

There are top loader kilns and front loader kilns and ones small enough to go on a workbench that are suitable for making jewellery. Modern electric glass kilns usually come supplied with a digital programmer, which means that you can set a complete firing cycle for your work (see also page 21).

It is possible to use a ceramic kiln, and in fact all the projects in this book were fired in two ceramic kilns.

This is because I found that it was much cheaper to buy a second-hand ceramic kiln than a glass kiln. I did make sure that the kilns were in good working order and I acquired programmers for each one.

If you do use a ceramic kiln you will need to do some test firings to find out what happens to the glass when it is fired in different places in the kiln. You will also need to make sure the kiln is clean inside, as you will not want ceramic powder sticking to your glasswork.

KILN SHELVES, KILN FURNITURE AND MOULDS

You can buy a range of kiln shelves in different shapes and sizes. They are made from high-fired clay and will need treating with shelf primer before use to prevent glass sticking to the surface. Alternatively you can buy Thinfire shelf paper to line the kiln shelf, though you can only use this paper once as it turns to dust during the firing.

Kiln supports are used to raise the shelves off the floor of the kiln and to support work in the kiln during firing.

The moulds used for the projects in this book are all made specifically for slumping glass. They have a very smooth surface and, if handled carefully, will last a long time. They need to be treated with shelf primer before use.

ABOVE *grozing pliers*
RIGHT *circle cutter*

ABOVE *glass glue*

GLASS

There are many different types of glass used for making kiln-formed pieces and you may be familiar with the terms 'float', 'Bullseye', 'Spectrum', 'Uroboros' and 'dichroic'. All of the projects in this book are made with Bullseye fusing glass, but there is no reason why you should not substitute other makes of fusing glass, though you will need to make sure that the glass is compatible (see page 14).

You will also find that glass comes in different forms: a selection of the most popular are listed here.

SHEET GLASS

This comes in a variety of different thicknesses and sizes; 3mm (³⁄₃₂ in.) is the usual thickness for the base glass. It is available as clear glass and in a myriad of colours.

Projects in this book are made using both transparent and opalescent coloured glass. Some also use 'striker' glass, which changes colour once it has been fired.

ABOVE *clear sheet glass*
RIGHT *coloured sheet glass*

ABOVE *glass stringers in a variety of colours*

FRITS AND POWDERS

Frits are small pieces of glass that are available in a range of grades from coarse through to powder.

STRINGERS

These are long 'strings' of glass that are available in different thicknesses. They are used for decoration or fine details on a piece of work.

RODS

Glass rods can be cut into slices and fused to base glass to make coloured dots on a project.

CONFETTI

Confetti is made from very thin glass. It shatters very easily but the small shards can look interesting as added texture on a piece of work.

DICHROIC GLASS

The 'di' of dichroic means two: this special glass both transmits and reflects colour. It's available in a range of colours, textures and patterns.

The glass is coated with a chemical film in a controlled environment and is costly to produce, which is why it is mainly used for making jewellery and to add accents in larger pieces.

OTHER TYPES OF GLASS

There are some other types of glass that are interesting to experiment with:

Iridescent glass – a glass with a surface coating that gives the appearance of a metallic sheen.

Decorative glass – this has frits and stringers incorporated in the glass during the manufacturing process.

Streakies – glass made with more than one colour for a streaked effect.

BELOW LEFT TO RIGHT *confetti, coarse frits and glass rods*
OPPOSITE *various types of dichroic glass*

COMPATIBILITY AND COEFFICIENT OF EXPANSION

It is very important that the types of glass you are proposing to use for fusing are compatible with one another. All fusing glass has a coefficient of expansion, or COE number, that refers to the rate at which the glass expands and contracts when it is heated and cooled; the viscosity of the glass also plays a part in compatibility.

If you use two types of glass that are incompatible you will have problems with the glass cracking or even shattering. If you are not sure what kind of glass you are using, you can fire a sample strip and then view it through a polarising filter (available from glass suppliers), which will show up any stress in the glass: it appears as a white halo.

For more information on compatibility, take a look at the Bullseye website (see page 127), which has an excellent range of technical notes.

As mentioned earlier, all of the projects in this book were made using Bullseye glass and if you buy just one type of glass you should not run into any difficulties.

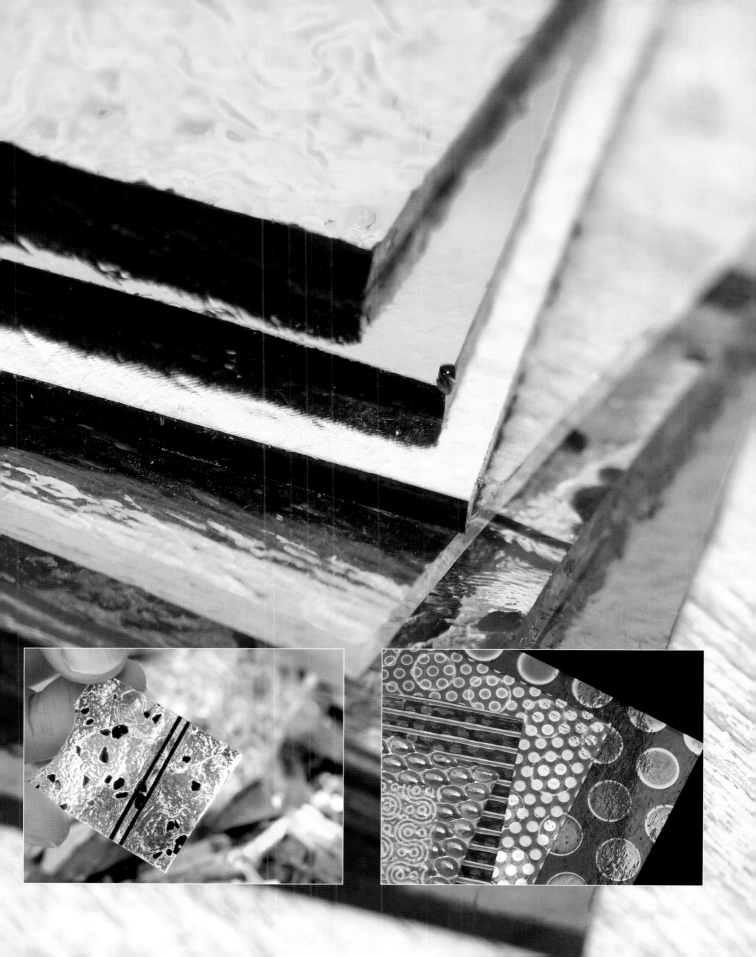

MATERIALS FOR INCLUSIONS

Inclusions are materials that can be sandwiched between layers of glass and fired. It is possible to include a wide range of materials, though glass will not tolerate anything too thick and will crack if placed under too much strain.

You can use wire mesh, brass and aluminium (the latter will turn black when fired), plus organic materials such as twigs and leaves, which leave behind a carbon imprint on firing.

BELOW *craft punch, copper wire, copper sheet, gold and silver leaf, silver wire*

COPPER

Copper is commonly used as an inclusion in kiln-formed glasswork. It will change colour during firing, but the nature of the change is very unpredictable. In this book copper wire is used for making hangers, but it can also be used for decorative purposes. You can use tinned copper wire if you wish, but remember that the tinning will burn off leaving the copper wire underneath. Copper sheet can be easily cut into different shapes or you can use a craft punch to make shapes.

GOLD LEAF

This is a metal that will retain its colour when heated, but the leaf can be fairly difficult to work with as it is very fragile.

SILVER LEAF

Silver leaf is less expensive than gold leaf. It also retains its colour when heated and can be a beautiful embellishment on a pendant.

OTHER SPECIAL EFFECT PRODUCTS

BUBBLE EFFECT POWDER

This is a strongly pigmented enamel that creates bubbles when used between layers of glass. There are several colours available.

ABOVE *glassline pens*

ABOVE *bubble effect powder*

ABOVE *glassline paper*

ABOVE *fibre rope*

GLASSLINE PENS

This is a range of versatile glass paints that can be used either on the surface of a piece of glass or between layers of glass.

Metal tips are available that fit onto the nozzles of the bottles of paint, allowing you to create a range of line thicknesses.

The paints can also be thinned with water and applied to glass with a brush or diffuser.

MICA

This is a mineral that is available in flake or powder form. It is used to give sparkle to glasswork, either on the surface or between layers of glass. It can also be mixed with enamel and painted on with a brush.

GLASSLINE PAPER

Glassline paper is a fusible paper that can be used between layers of glass and can also be drawn on using glassline pens.

FIBRE PAPER AND FIBRE ROPE

Fibre paper is made from vitreous aluminosilicate fibres and is specially designed for use with kiln-formed glass techniques.

Thinfire paper is used for lining kiln shelves as an alternative to using shelf primer. Each sheet is only used for one firing because it burns up.

Thicker fibre paper, ranging from 3–6mm (³⁄₃₂–¼ in.) thick, can be used to create texture in glass by cutting or tearing the paper and placing it

under the base glass. During firing the glass will form around the shapes made by the fibre paper.

Fibre rope can be used to create holes in glass by placing it between layers of glass. It can also be used in the same way as fibre paper to create texture in glass.

GLASS BEADS

Glass beads are easy to make and are a great way of using up scrap glass. Simply cut the glass into small squares, or slice up pieces of rod, place them on a prepared kiln shelf and fire them at full fuse temperature. Each square or slice will turn into a bead. You could also try stacking two or three squares together to make larger beads.

ABOVE *slices of glass rods and finished glass beads*

BASIC
TECHNIQUES

CUTTING TIPS

Cutting glass always seems a little daunting when you first start, but once you have overcome your initial fears it will soon be a relatively straightforward process.

You will need to buy a good glass cutter (see page 11) and it will be useful to have a cutting square. It is easier to cut glass standing up, so check that your work surface is the right height for this.

Make sure the glass is clean, then measure and mark the shape using a fine marker pen. The glass may be smoother on one side and it is easier to cut on this smoother side.

Cut along the marked line in a smooth, firm movement, maintaining an even pressure and without lifting the cutter off the glass until you reach the other edge. This takes practice and it is worth doing some trials on spare pieces of glass.

You should be able to see a fine score line after cutting. If the glass has not scored properly, do not go over the cut again as this will not work. Instead you could try cutting it again on the other side.

Once scored, the glass should be broken straight away using grozing pliers (see page 12). Hold the glass with the pliers and break it with one firm movement: with practice you should be able to get a clean break.

Make sure any small pieces of glass are brushed off the work surface before continuing. I keep a plastic box for table 'sweepings'.

CIRCLES

Circles can be cut freehand or you can use a circle cutter (see page 12), which works in a similar way to ordinary compasses.

You can buy pre-cut glass circles, but you may not always be able to buy the size you require. All the projects in this book requiring circles can be made with pre-cut circles.

If you are using a circle cutter, score the circle first and then make a straight line score from the edge of the glass to the circle. Score three or four straight lines at different places around the circle.

Tap the underside of the glass using the 'wrong' end of your glass cutter on the score lines and you should be able to remove the pieces around the circle in sections.

CUTTING INSIDE CURVES

Start by drawing and then scoring the shape. Then score straight lines across from the edge of the glass. Tap the glass underneath and remove the broken glass using grozing pliers.

LEFT *cutting glass*
BELOW *glass circles*

GRINDING

Before you use a grinder, check the water level and ensure that the sponge is wet before you start; this keeps the grinding head from overheating. Always wear eye protection to prevent glass particles getting in your eyes.

Grinding can discolour the edges of glass; this is not always noticeable but can be avoided if you keep grinding to a minimum. You can use a light application of devitrification spray on the edges if you wish.

CLEANING GLASS

Dust and grease can cause glass to devitrify during firing. This gives the surface a whitish appearance and can spoil the finished piece. It is possible to use a devitrification spray to prevent this happening.

Clean the glass with vinegar, glass cleaner or water containing a little detergent, then dry it with lint-free paper towels. Pen marks can be removed with alcohol.

Once your glass project is fired, you can remove the fibre paper residue by washing the glass with water and detergent. This also helps stop the fibre dust from being released into the atmosphere.

PREPARING THE KILN FOR FIRING

If you have a new kiln it should have instructions on kiln preparation. However, a second-hand kiln may not have come with any paperwork.

Start by vacuuming the kiln to remove any dust, then protect the kiln floor with kiln wash. This is also known as shelf primer and is powder that is mixed with water then applied with a soft brush. Apply three or four coats, brushing in different directions for each coat, then allow to dry for

about a day. This protective layer will prevent pieces of glass adhering to the floor and damaging to your kiln.

You will also need to prime your kiln shelves, unless you have decided to use shelf paper. If you prime kiln shelves, you will need to reapply primer from time to time, but remove the old primer with a paint scraper first (remembering to wear a mask).

When you place your kiln shelf in the kiln, it is important to use kiln posts to raise the shelf off the floor so that air can circulate during firing.

PREPARING MOULDS FOR FIRING

All of the slumped projects in this book are made using clay moulds and these need to be prepared for firing.

1 | Mix the up kiln wash.

2 | Using a soft brush, such as a haike brush, apply four coats to the mould, applying each coat at right angles to the previous one.

3 | Dry the prepared mould for about 20 minutes in the kiln at 200°C/400°F.

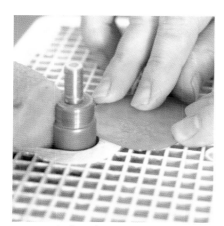

ABOVE *grinding glass*

THE FUSING

AND SLUMPING PROCESS

The term 'fusing' refers to the process of heating compatible pieces of glass until they fuse together. This takes place in the environment of the kiln, where the heating and cooling process is carefully controlled.

There are different degrees of fusing: tack fusing is when the glass is fired to a point where pieces stick together, but are only just beginning to soften at the edges. Full fusing is when glass is heated enough for the pieces to merge fully into one. The piece below right is tack fused; you can see that the squares and triangles of glass have distinct edges.

Below left is the same piece fully fused. The edges of the separate sections of glass have merged. Also, notice how the colours vary with the temperature of firing.

Most fusing glass will begin to fuse at 718°C/1325°F, but the rate at which glass reaches full fuse will depend on the thickness of the glass and the number of layers you are firing. You may have to make some adjustments to suit your kiln.

Slumping refers to the placing of an already-fired piece of glass over a mould and then firing it again until it droops and takes the shape of the mould.

RIGHT *the tack fused piece and* INSET RIGHT *the fully fused piece.*

FIRING STAGES

There are up to five stages in a firing cycle, though they will vary.

1 INITIAL HEATING PHASE
The glass is heated from room temperature to the strain point (the point at which the glass is still a solid), somewhere between 500–540°C/930–1000°F.

2 RAPID HEATING PHASE
538C–816°C/1000–1500°F for fusing or 538–700°C/1000–1300°F for slumping. The glass is heated rapidly to the required top temperature. This is then held (soaked) for 5 to 30 minutes.

3 ANNEALING SOAK PHASE
From 510–399°C/950–750°F. Annealing is the process during which glass returns to a solid form. The time needed for this varies with different types of glass, but as long as the glass has plenty of time to go through this stage there should not be a risk of thermal shock, which is when glass cracks due to either being heated or cooled too quickly.

4 RAPID COOLING PHASE
The kiln is allowed to cool. This can be by done leaving it to cool down naturally, though some glass artists open the kiln door briefly to allow hot air to escape. This speeds up the process, but you must wear gloves and safety goggles to do this.

5 COOL TO ROOM TEMPERATURE PHASE
399°C/750°F to room temperature. This is usually a matter of just allowing the kiln to cool down naturally. However, be aware that this may take time if you are firing thick pieces or if your kiln retains the heat.

FIRING SCHEDULES

The following schedules are recommended for tack fusing, full fusing and slump firing Bullseye glass, which is the kind I used in this book.

However, you should follow the directions that come with your kiln and do some practice firings to see how your kiln behaves. Keep a notebook in which you write down your observations; for example, type of firing, all the details of the firing times and temperatures, plus comments on the results. This can be a very useful tool when you are aiming to reproduce a piece of work at a later date.

SAMPLE SCHEDULE FOR TACK FUSE FIRING

(of one layer of 4mm (⅛ in.) base glass and an application of frits and powders)

Step	Rate (degrees per hour)	Temperature	Hold
1 Initial heat	333°C/600°F	691–788°C/1275–1450°F	10 mins
Process soak			
2 Rapid cool	AFAP*	516°C/960°F	1 hour
Anneal soak			
3 Anneal cool	55°C/100°F	371°C/700°F	00 mins
4 Final cool	AFAP	21°C/70°F	00 mins

* As fast as possible

SAMPLE SCHEDULE FOR FULL FUSE FIRING

(a piece 30.5cm (12 in.) diameter with two layers 3mm (3/32 in.) glass)

Step	Rate (degrees per hour)	Temperature	Hold
1 Initial heat	222°C/400°F	677°C/1250°F	30 mins
Pre-rapid heat soak			
2 Rapid heat	333°C/600°F	804°C/1480°F	10 mins
Process soak			
3 Rapid cool	AFAP	516°C/960°F	30 mins
Anneal soak			
4 Anneal cool	83°C/150°F	371°C/700°F	00 mins
5 Final cool	AFAP	21°C/70°F	00 mins

SAMPLE SCHEDULE FOR SLUMP FIRING

(for same piece as above)

Step	Rate (degrees per hour)	Temperature	Hold
1 Initial heat	166°C/300°F	638°C/1180°F	10 mins
Process soak			
2 Rapid cool	AFAP	516°C/960°F	1 hour
Anneal soak			
3 Anneal cool	55°C/100°F	371°C/700°F	00 mins
4 Final cool	AFAP	21°C/70°F	00 mins

PROBLEM
SOLVING

DEVITRIFICATION

As mentioned earlier in the section on cleaning glass (page 19), devitrification can be a problem, especially with certain types of glass. Apart from grease and dirt on the glass, it can also be caused by being kept too long at around 700°C/ 1300°F, which is just below the point at which glass becomes molten. You can use devitrification spray, but the glass must be dry before firing.

BUBBLES

Bubbles are formed during firing for many different reasons and you may or may not like them in your work. Most commonly they will appear between layers of glass. It is difficult to resolve this problem completely, but using smaller pieces of glass can help. Anything that causes pockets of air to be trapped can potentially create bubbles – for example, wire inclusions between layers.

Sometimes very large bubbles are formed; these are created by gases that cannot escape during the firing process. You could try soaking the glass at 600°C/1100°F for about half an hour to resolve this problem.

MISSHAPEN SLUMPED PIECES

During a slump firing you may find that the glass is not able to drop down into the mould. This is caused by the air holes in the mould being blocked by kiln wash and can easily be cured by ensuring the holes are clear before using the mould.

CRACKS

One of the most frequent reasons for cracks is that more than one type of glass has been used to make the piece and they are not compatible.

ABOVE *a pendant and a fish placed too close together have fused in the kiln*

This should not be a problem if you work only with glass guaranteed to be compatible (see page 14). Sometimes cracking is due to improper annealing (see page 20) and it may be necessary to increase the length of time for this stage.

TOO MUCH GLUE

You may find black spots inside your glass. This is caused by using too much glass glue or by waiting too long before firing the piece. Use the minimum amount of glue possible and fire the work as soon as you can.

STICKING TOGETHER

Don't forget that you need plenty of space between projects in the kiln or they will fuse together.

TOP LEFT *bubbles in glass*

BELOW LEFT *black spots caused by too much glass glue*

RIGHT *a misshapen slumped dish*

DISPLAY

Most of the flat panel projects in this book are displayed by the simple means of including a wire hook during the construction. However, you could drill holes in your panel or glue a stand-off to the back of your work.

For drilling holes you can buy an attachment called a flex shaft that fits onto the head of the grinder and to which a diamond wire drill can be attached.

Stand-offs are cylindrical aluminium wall mounts that are glued onto the back of the glass and then slotted into a bracket attached to the wall. The effect is to display the glass a short distance from the wall. These are made in a variety of sizes and are available from most glass suppliers.

Simple acrylic stands designed for displaying plates are easily obtainable in a range of sizes and can look very effective. This is probably the easiest way to display your work and you can try different settings to see how the light changes the look of your glasswork.

PROJECTS

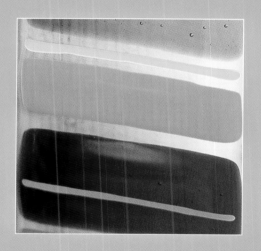

YOU'LL FIND A WIDE RANGE OF PROJECTS TO MAKE IN THIS BOOK. THERE ARE SIMPLE FLAT PIECES THAT ARE IDEAL STARTER PROJECTS IF YOU HAVE DONE VERY LITTLE WORK WITH GLASS. AS YOU GAIN SKILLS AND CONFIDENCE YOU'LL WANT TO MOVE ON TO THE MORE COMPLEX PIECES.

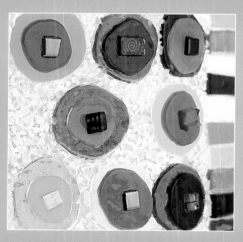

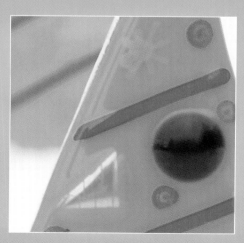

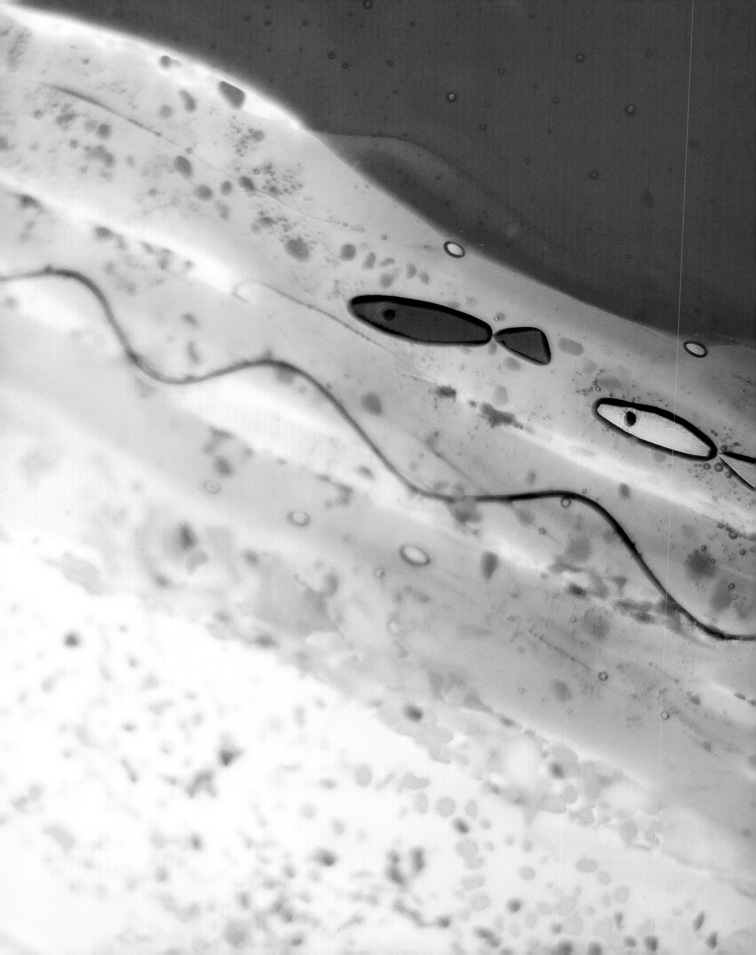

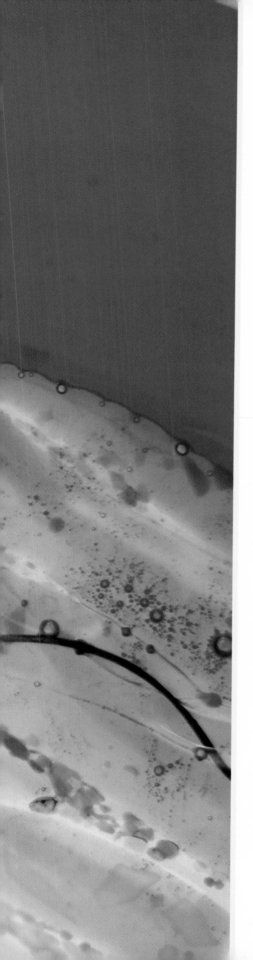

FLAT
PIECES

THESE ARE THE SIMPLEST TYPES OF GLASS PROJECTS, BUT ALTHOUGH THEY ARE EASY TO MAKE, THEY ARE STILL SATISFYING TO WORK ON AND BEAUTIFUL TO LOOK AT.

PATTERNED

COASTERS

EQUIPMENT
this is the same for all the coasters
unless otherwise stated
- Safety goggles
- Cutting surface
- Oil-filled glass cutter
- Grozing pliers
- Jewellery pliers
- Scribe
- Glue brush
- Dry paintbrush
- Cutting square
- Ruler
- Fine marker pen
- Paper towels
- Vinegar or glass cleaner
- Grinder
- Kiln

Coasters are an easy first project and there are many variations to be made. If you have not done any glass work before then the Striped Coaster (see opposite) and the Bubble Coaster (see page 30) are probably the easiest projects to make first. Once you have more experience of cutting glass, then you can go on to the floral coasters (see pages 32 and 34).

The starting point for all of the coasters is to cut a piece of 6mm (¼ in.) thick clear glass measuring 9.5 x 9.5cm (3¾ x 3¾ in.). This glass can be quite hard to cut, but it gives a good weight to the finished coaster. If you find the thicker glass problematic, you could use 4mm (⅛ in.) thick glass if you prefer. After firing, add a bumper stop to the corners of the coaster to prevent it from sliding on a polished surface.

STRIPED COASTER

*The method for making this coaster
is the same as for the Stripy Panel
(see page 36), but without the need
for a hanger.*

MATERIALS
- Clear fusing glass 6mm (¼ in.) thick
- Coloured fusing glass in sheets:
  Transparent 2mm (⅟₁₆ in.) thick in Fuchsia
  Pink, Red and Deep Plum
  Opalescent 2mm (⅟₁₆ in.) thick in Tomato
  Red and Pumpkin Orange
- Stringers 1mm (⅟₃₂ in.) in Orange, Red and
  dichroic
- Glass glue
- Thinfire shelf paper
- Self-adhesive bumper stops

1 | Measure and cut a 9.5cm (3¾ in.) strip of the 6mm (¼ in.) glass.

2 | If you find it hard to break the glass, you can tap along the line of the cut with the handle end of your cutter. Make sure that you hold the sheet of glass low to your cutting table in case it breaks suddenly. (Try not to do this too often when you are cutting glass as you sometimes get a ragged edge where the glass has not broken cleanly.)

BUBBLE COASTER

This coaster is easy to make and can be varied by using stringers of different colours or thickness. The square of glass laid on top will make bubbles form in the squares created by the stringers.

MATERIALS

- Clear fusing glass 6mm (¼ in.) thick
- Clear fusing glass 2mm (⅟₁₆ in.) thick
- Stringers 1mm (⅟₃₂ in.) in Red, Yellow, Blue and Orange
- Glass glue
- Thinfire shelf paper
- Self-adhesive bumper stops

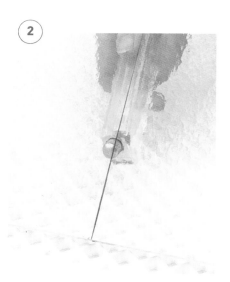

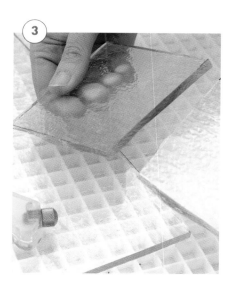

3 Measure and cut a 9.5cm (3¾ in.) square from the strip of glass.

4 Break the stringers into pieces the same width as the coaster.

5 Lay the stringers about 1cm (⅜ in.) apart on the coaster, alternating the colours. Glue in place using a small amount of glue.

6 Place another layer of stringers at 90 degrees to the first layer and glue them in place.

7 Place the square of thinner glass on the top. You may find that the stringers roll easily; if so you will need to check them again once the coaster is in the kiln.

8 Fire at full fuse firing (see page 21). Stick some bumper stops on the back of the coaster, one in each corner.

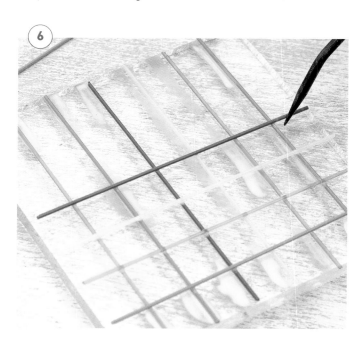

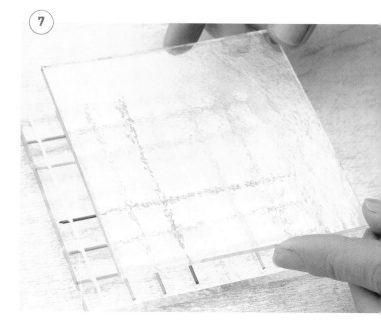

PASSIONFLOWER COASTER

I love the structure of passionflowers and thought it would be fun to try to make one in glass. It is a little more complicated than the other coasters, but well worth persevering with.

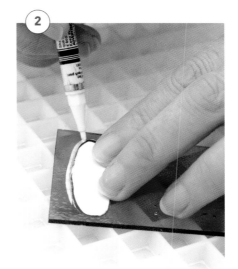

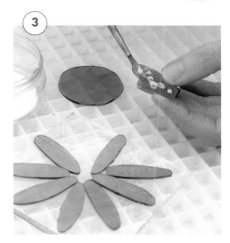

ADDITIONAL EQUIPMENT
- White marker pen

MATERIALS
- Clear fusing glass 6mm (¼ in.) thick
- Coloured fusing glass in sheets:
  Transparent 2mm (⅟₁₆ in.) thick in Fuchsia **Opalescent** 2mm (⅟₁₆ in.) thick in Spring Green
- Stringers 1mm (⅟₃₂ in.) in White opalescent
- Frits (medium) in Jade Green opalescent and Marigold Yellow transparent
- Glass glue
- Petal template (see page 124)
- Thinfire shelf paper
- Self-adhesive bumper stops

1 Cut 9.5cm (3¾ in.) squares of both thicknesses of clear glass, cutting the thick glass as for Steps 1–3 of the Bubble Coaster (see page 30).

2 Using the white pen, draw around the template ten times onto Fuchsia transparent. Cut out the petals and a circle 4.5cm (1¾ in.) in diameter. Grind off any rough edges if necessary.

3 Arrange the petals on the base glass and glue them in place. Glue the circle into the centre of the flower, on top of the petals.

4 To make the anthers of the flower, cut five strips of Spring Green opalescent, each about 1.5cm (⅝ in.) long. Glue them in place in a star shape, radiating out from the centre of the circle. Cut five small pieces of the same glass and glue one at right angles across the end of each arm of the star.

5 Brush a little glue on the remaining areas of clear glass and sprinkle on some frits to create a background texture. It's a good idea to lay the piece of work on a sheet of paper before sprinkling on the frits. Any excess will then be caught on the paper and can be returned to their container.

6 Add about 20 white opalescent stringers radiating out from the centre circle. Fire at a full fuse firing (see page 21).

7 After firing, stick some bumper stops on the back of the coaster, one in each corner.

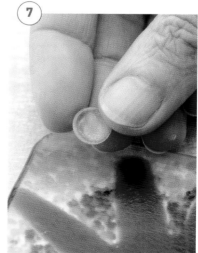

33

ADDITIONAL EQUIPMENT
- White marker pen

MATERIALS
- Clear fusing glass 6mm
  (¼ in.) thick
- Coloured fusing glass in sheets:
  Opalescent 2mm (¹⁄₁₆ in.) in
  Marigold Yellow, Spring Green
  and Jade Green
- Small pieces of transparent 2mm
  (¹⁄₁₆ in.) glass in different shades
  of blue
- Glass glue
- Petal and leaf templates
  (see page 124)
- Thinfire shelf paper
- Self-adhesive bumper stops

TULIP COASTER

Tulips are a lovely subject for glass work; their simple forms are very effective and you could make a set of coasters in different colours. The background of this coaster is made from lots of small pieces of scrap glass.

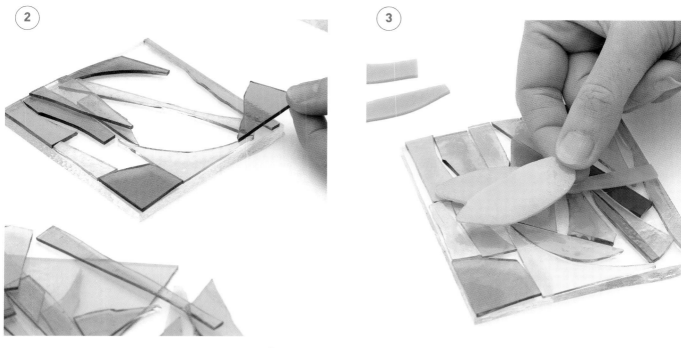

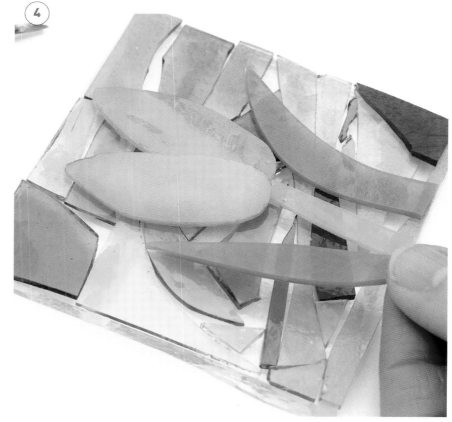

1 Cut a 9.5cm (3¾ in.) square of clear glass, cutting the thick glass as for Steps 1–3 of the Bubble Coaster (see page 30).

2 Using small pieces of different shades of blue transparent glass off cuts (make sure they are washed before you use them), cover the clear glass square. Glue all the pieces into place.

3 Using the templates and white pen, trace and cut out two petals from the Marigold Yellow opalescent glass. Cut two leaves from the Jade Green opalescent and a stem to fit out of the Spring Green opalescent.

4 Glue all the pieces in place. Fire at full fuse firing (see page 21). Stick some bumper stops on the back of the coaster, one in each corner.

STRIPY
PANEL

MATERIALS
- Clear fusing glass 3mm (³⁄₃₂ in.) thick measuring 21 x 5.5cm (8¼ x 2¼ in.)
- Coloured fusing glass in sheets: **Transparent** 2mm (¹⁄₁₆ in.) thick in Fuchsia Pink, Red and Deep Plum **Opalescent** 2mm (¹⁄₁₆ in.) thick in Tomato Red and Pumpkin Orange
- Stringers 1mm (¹⁄₃₂ in.) in Orange, Red and dichroic
- Glass glue
- 18-gauge copper wire
- Thinfire shelf paper
- Ribbon for hanging

EQUIPMENT
- Safety goggles
- Cutting surface
- Oil-filled glass cutter
- Grozing pliers
- Jewellery pliers
- Scribe
- Glue brush
- Cutting square
- Ruler
- Fine black marker pen
- Wire cutters
- Paper towels
- Vinegar or glass cleaner
- Grinder
- Kiln

These simple panels look great if you make several in different colours and hang them on a pale wall. You could also try making them different lengths, depending on the size of your kiln of course.

1 Cut pieces of transparent and opalescent glass to fit the width of the clear base piece. Make the panel more interesting by varying the depth of each coloured stripe. For the hanger, cut a piece of copper wire about 5cm (2 in.) long, bend it into a hook and glue it to the front of the base glass, at the top. Glue a fairly wide piece of glass on the top (use opalescent glass if you do not want to see the hook).

2 Add stringers in a range of colours and thicknesses. Using dichroic stringers costs a bit more, but they add a shimmer to your work. They do not always stay straight when fired, an effect you may or may not like! Fire the panel at full fuse firing or at tack fuse temperature (see page 21) if you prefer a more textured piece of work.

FLOWER PANELS

These are half the width of the Stripy Panel and feature a floral design. Turn to the Small Round Flower Dish project (see page 84) for ideas and techniques for making the various flowers.

BLUE RUG
PANEL

MATERIALS
- Clear fusing glass 3mm (³⁄₃₂ in.) thick measuring 21.5 x 6cm (8½ x 2½ in.)
- Coloured fusing glass in sheets: **Opalescent** 2mm (¹⁄₁₆ in.) thick in Cobalt Blue and selection of 2cm (¾ in.) squares in shades of blue **Transparent** 2mm (¹⁄₁₆ in.) thick selection of 1.8cm (¾ in.) squares in shades of blue
- 6 small squares of dichroic glass
- Glass glue
- 18-gauge copper wire
- Thinfire shelf paper
- Ribbon for hanging

EQUIPMENT
- Safety goggles
- Cutting surface
- Oil-filled glass cutter
- Grozing pliers
- Jewellery pliers
- Scribe
- Glue brush
- Cutting square
- Ruler
- Fine black marker pen
- Wire cutters
- Paper towels
- Vinegar or glass cleaner
- Grinder
- Kiln

Inspired by woven kelims, these rug panels take quite a lot of time and patience to make, but they are very beautiful. They are also a good way to make use of small pieces of scrap glass and several could be made in a range of different colours.

This project shows you the basic principles of constructing a rug panel, but this really is a design where the results will be dictated by your own imagination and, of course, what colours of scrap glass you have. You can also include bits of rod, stringer and confetti in your panels (see page 41).

1

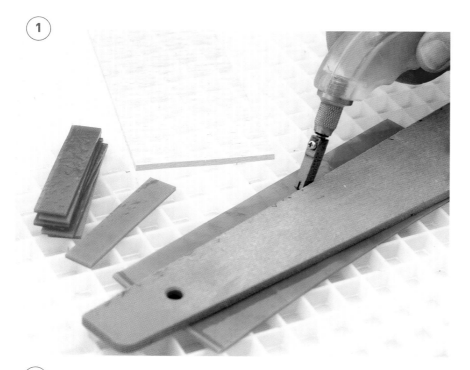

1 Using the cutting square, cut strips of Cobalt Blue glass measuring 1.3cm (½ in.) wide.

2 Cut the strips of Cobalt Blue to fit the width of the base. Arrange them on the base panel spacing them 1.8cm (¾ in.) apart, with a slightly wider gap between the top strip and the next one down.

3 Cut a piece of the copper wire about 10cm (4 in.) long and bend it into a hook. Glue it to the front of the panel, at the top, and then glue a piece of Cobalt Blue over the top. Arrange squares of transparent glass in rows of three across the base piece between the strips of Cobalt Blue, mixing different shades of blue.

2

3

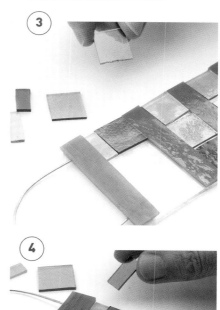

4

4 | Cut some small rectangles of glass to fit below the first strip of Cobalt Blue.

5 | Glue a square of opalescent blue glass in the centre of each transparent square.

6 | Finally, glue a small square of dichroic glass in the centre of each middle square. Fire either at tack fusing or full fusing temperature (see page 21).

RUG VARIATIONS

Try experimenting with alternate layers of thin strips of glass and stringers, with additional lines of carefully applied frits. This works especially well if you limit your design to two or three colours, or to different tones of the same colour.

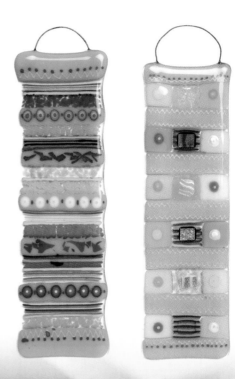

# DRAGONFLY
BELL PANEL

MATERIALS
- Clear fusing glass 3mm (³∕₃₂ in.) thick measuring approx 13 x 11.5cm (5¼ x 4½ in.)
- Coloured fusing glass in sheets: **Transparent** 2mm (¹∕₁₆ in.) thick in Sea Blue, Pine Green, Aqua Blue and small pieces of different blues for the water
- Frits (medium) in Turquoise transparent and Turquoise opalescent
- Dichroic Aurora Borealis Cool on thin black, Ripple Emerald on black, Savoy Sand Art on thin clear and Radium Ripple Rainbow 2 on clear
- Dichroic stringer in clear
- Glass glue
- 18-gauge copper wire
- Thinfire shelf paper
- Ribbon for hanging

EQUIPMENT
- Safety goggles
- Cutting surface
- Oil-filled glass cutter
- Grozing pliers
- Jewellery pliers
- Scribe
- Glue brush
- Dry paintbrush
- Fine black marker pen
- White marker pen
- Wire cutters
- Paper towels
- Vinegar or glass cleaner
- Grinder
- Kiln
- Template (see page 124)

The shape of this panel came about because I saw some windows that were bell-shaped and thought that it would make a great format for a glass panel. I experimented and loved the results. This dragonfly panel looks beautiful hung on a light-coloured wall, but would be equally lovely hung in a window.

I live in an area where there are a lot of streams and so dragonflies are frequent visitors during the summer months. Their glorious flashes of turquoise and green caught my eye and I felt compelled to try to capture their beauty. Dichroic glass is an ideal medium for showing off the dragonfly's shimmering body and wings. There are lots of variations you could try, including using different-patterned glass for the dragonfly's wings or changing the colours in the background.

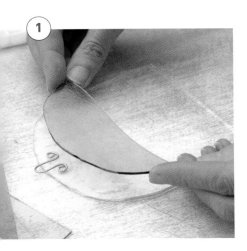

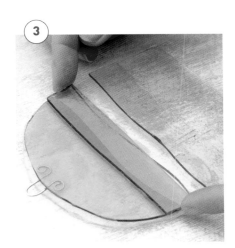

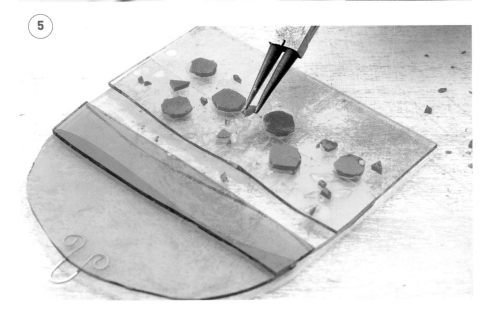

1   Start this panel in the same way as the Dragonfly Bell Panel (see page 44) by cutting the base glass and making a wire hook. Cut out the sky piece from Turquoise transparent glass. Glue the hook in place on the base at the top of the panel the lay the sky piece over it.

2   Cut a piece of Light Amber transparent glass that fits the width of the base and is about 3cm (1½ in.) in depth. Glue this in the centre of the base. Cut a piece of transparent Sunflower Yellow glass so that it fits the bottom half of the base and overlaps the Light Amber piece.

3   Cut a piece of Spring Green transparent that overlaps both the Turquoise and the Light Amber glass. Glue all these pieces in place.

4   Make the poppies by cutting some small squares of Red opalescent glass. Use the grozing pliers to break off bits to create uneven shapes. (Broken-off pieces can be sprinkled onto the centre of the panel to create the effect of

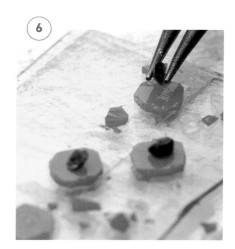

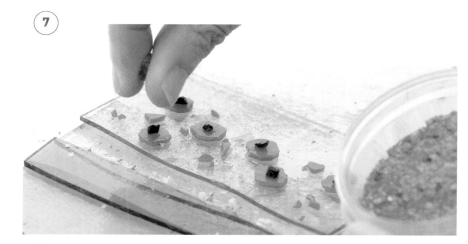

more poppies. Add dabs of glue before sprinkling.)

5   Glue the poppies onto the panel.

6   Using dabs of glue to hold them in place, add some Deep Royal Purple coarse frits for the centres of the poppies.

7   Dab a little glue onto the bottom half of the panel and add a few Red opalescent frits to create an effect of more poppies in the distance. Add some Canary Yellow opalescent frits to create the effect of corn.

8   Add some green stringers for grass in the foreground. Draw on some poppy stems with the Green Glassline pen and some corn stems with the Gold Glassline pen. Fire either at tack fuse or full fuse temperature (see page 21).

# GARDEN

BY THE SEA PANEL

MATERIALS

- Clear fusing glass 2mm (⅟₁₆ in.) thick measuring 25 x 19cm (10 x 7½ in.)
- Coloured fusing glass in sheets:
  Transparent 2mm (⅟₁₆ in.) thick in Light Sky Blue, Deep Royal Blue, Turquoise, Light Amber and Pine Green
  Opalescent 2mm (⅟₁₆ in.) thick in Mineral Green, Teal Green and White
- Stringers 1mm (⅟₃₂ in.) in Green
- Frits (medium) in Sunflower Yellow transparent, Cinnabar opalescent and White opalescent
- Frits (coarse) in Deep Royal Purple, Medium Marigold Yellow transparent, White translucent, Teal Green opalescent, Green transparent and Purple
- Confetti in White and Orange
- Rods in Marigold Yellow and Red
- 18-gauge copper wire
- Blue Bubble Effect powder
- Glass glue
- Fibre paper 3mm (³⁄₃₂ in.) thick
- Thinfire shelf paper

A garden on a hill overlooking the sea was the source of inspiration for this decorative panel. The waves in the sea are made from strips of fibre paper that are placed directly on the lined kiln shelf before firing. The glass will then form around the shapes and create indentations in the finished panel. You can have a lot of fun creating the foliage in the foreground by choosing different colours of glass for the flowers, or by using Glassline pens to draw shapes onto the surface.

EQUIPMENT

- Safety goggles
- Cutting surface
- Oil-filled glass cutter
- Grozing pliers
- Jewellery pliers
- Scissors
- Scribe
- Glue brush
- Dry paintbrush
- Cutting square
- Ruler
- Fine black marker pen
- Wire cutters
- Vinegar or glass cleaner
- Paper towels
- Grinder
- Kiln
- Templates (see page 125)

1 Using the templates, trace and cut the glass for the sky from Light Sky Blue, the horizon from Deep Royal Blue, the sea from Turquoise, the beach from Light Amber and the foreground from Pine Green.

2 Place the pieces on the base glass and check that they fit neatly together. You may need to cut or grind some pieces to fit.

3 Cut two lengths of copper wire, each about 10cm (4 in.) long, and bend them into hooks, curling the ends around using pliers.

4 Glue the hooks in place at the top of the panel, then glue the sky piece over the top of them.

5 Glue the horizon piece in place below the sky.

6 Using a dry brush, put a little blue Bubble Effect powder onto the base glass where the Turquoise transparent glass will lie. The powder will create small bubbles in the Turquoise sea, but take care not to use too much or it will create blisters.

7 Now gently place the Turquoise transparent glass over the top of the powder. Glue in place the Light Amber beach and the Pine Green foreground.

8 Using some off-cuts of the Pine Green, trace shapes to fit the gaps on either side of the sea.

9 | Cut out the traced pieces and glue them in place.

10 | Cut some long pieces of Mineral Green opalescent glass for pine tree branches and glue them on the top right-hand side of the panel.

11 | Cut some long, thin Teal Green opalescent pieces for grass, some White opalescent petals for two daisies and a piece of Yellow rod for the centre of each daisy. Glue all these pieces in place.

12 Using grozing pliers, break some Orange confetti into random shapes and glue them on the left-hand side of the panel.

13 Glue some green stringers to the bottom of the panel to look like grass.

14 Now you can create some texture and more colour by adding frits and pieces of rod to create foliage on either side of the panel. Brush a little glue onto the shoreline and the beach and add some broken pieces of White confetti and White frits to look like crashing waves. Add some Sunflower Yellow, Cinnabar and White frits to create texture on the beach. Sprinkle Teal Green frits among the foliage.

15 To create extra texture in the sea, cut out wave shapes from the 3mm (³⁄₃₂ in.) fibre paper.

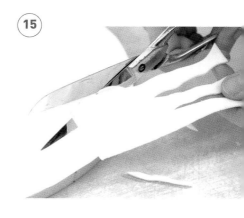

16 Place the fibre paper waves onto the lined kiln shelf where the sea section of the panel will lie. The glass will form around the fibre paper during the firing to create indentations in the sea.

17 Check that all the pieces are in the right place and fire either at full fuse or tack fuse if you prefer your panel to have more texture (see page 21).

BEACH SCENE VARIATION

This panel (right) puts more emphasis on creating texture in the sea using scrap glass and frits. The copper wire wave is held in place between the base and the coloured glass. The fish are made from tiny pieces of dichroic glass cut to shape.

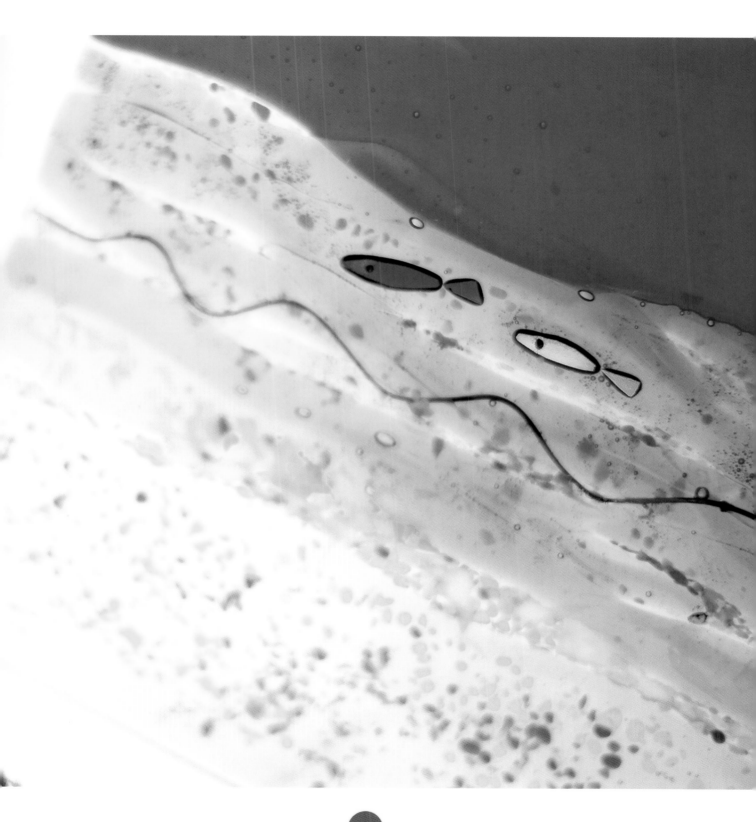

# HOUSE
NUMBER PANEL

MATERIALS

- Circle of 3mm (³⁄₃₂ in.) clear glass 23cm (9 in.) in diameter
- 2mm (¹⁄₁₆ in.) thick clear glass offcuts
- Fibre paper 6mm (¼ in.) and 3mm (³⁄₃₂ in.) thick
- Turquoise Blue transparent glass
- Small pieces of 2mm (¹⁄₁₆ in.) thick different-coloured glass
- Copper sheet
- 20-gauge copper wire
- Glassline pens in Dark Blue, Red Orange, White and Gold.
- Glitter Bronze mica powder
- Thinfire shelf paper

EQUIPMENT

- Safety goggles
- Cutting surface
- Oil-filled glass cutter
- Grozing pliers
- Jewellery pliers
- Scissors
- Scribe
- Sun motif paper punch
- Compasses
- Fine mesh sieve
- Dust mask
- Glue brush
- Fine black marker pen
- Paper towels
- Vinegar or glass cleaner
- Grinder
- Kiln

For this project you will need to work directly on the kiln shelf to avoid moving the fibre paper numbers that are placed underneath the circle of glass. For the numbers, choose a font on your computer that is fairly clear because the design requires you to trace the numbers onto fibre paper and cut them out. The numbers illustrated are Century Gothic, font size 300, printed in outline. If you need more than two numbers on your panel, reduce the size of them to fit into the inner circle.

The copper sheet and wire inclusions add interest to this project; you will notice that the copper changes colour and that there will probably be air bubbles trapped in the spirals of wire.

1 Line the kiln shelf with a piece of Thinfire shelf paper. Place the circle of clear glass on top and draw around it using the fine black pen.

2 Remove the glass, measure and mark the centre of the circle on the Thinfire paper and on the glass.

3 Trace the numbers onto the 6mm (¼ in.) fibre paper and cut them out.

4 Using compasses, draw a 14cm (5½ in.) diameter circle on the Thinfire paper, inside the first circle. Now draw a circle the same size on the transparent Turquoise glass; you can do this either by placing the glass on the Thinfire paper and tracing the circle with a pen, or you can draw the circle on thin paper and then trace onto the glass using graphite paper. Cut out the circle of glass.

5 Grind off any sharp edges.

6 Place the fibre paper numbers in the small circle on the Thinfire paper. Cut out some stars from the 3mm (⅛ in.) fibre paper and place them in the outer circle, but slightly overlapping the edge into the inner circle. (You could find a template for the stars but I think they look better cut freehand so that they are not symmetrical.)

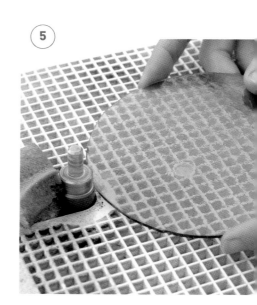

5

6

7

7 Place the clear circle of glass on top of the numbers and stars so that the edge lines up with the large drawn circle. Glue the smaller circle of Turquoise glass into the centre of the larger circle. Using the sun paper punch, cut out some suns from copper sheet.

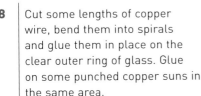

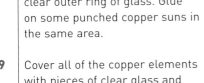

8 Cut some lengths of copper wire, bend them into spirals and glue them in place on the clear outer ring of glass. Glue on some punched copper suns in the same area.

9 Cover all of the copper elements with pieces of clear glass and glue them in place – the pieces of glass need to be big enough to cover each spiral or sun.

10 Cut out triangles of different colours of glass. Make them different sizes (maximum 2cm (¾ in.) long) and glue them in place around the rim.

11 Using a White Glassline pen with a medium nib, outline the fibre paper numbers. Leave until dry. If you have a turntable, you may find it easier to put the kiln shelf on it for this step.

12 Using a fine sieve, sprinkle a small amount of mica powder around the rim. This powder is very fine and you should wear a dust mask to avoid inhaling it.

13 Decorate the numbers with dots of various sizes using the Red and Blue Glassline pens.

14 Outline the stars with the Gold Glassline pen. Once the paint is dry, fire at tack fuse temperature (see page 21).

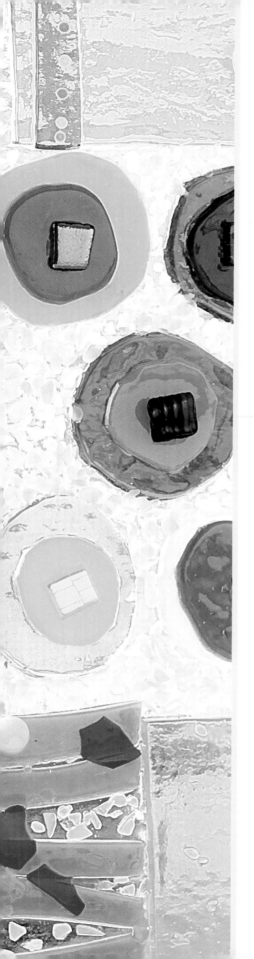

FRAMED
AND SLUMPED PIECES

ONCE YOU HAVE GAINED CONFIDENCE MAKING FLAT PANELS, MOVE ON TO THREE-DIMENSIONAL GLASS PIECES. THESE ARE MADE BY A PROCESS CALLED 'SLUMPING' IN WHICH PREVIOUSLY FIRED PIECES ARE GIVEN A SECOND FIRING OVER A MOULD. YOU CAN EASILY CREATE THE MOST BEAUTIFUL DISHES THIS WAY.

SQUARE
MIRROR FRAME

MATERIALS

- Mirror glass measuring 14 x 14cm (5½ x 5½ in.), available from a local glass supplier; if you are cutting it yourself cut it on the back, or buy a mirror tile the right size
- Clear fusing glass 3mm (³⁄₃₂ in.) thick, two strips measuring 20 x 4cm (8 x 1½ in.) and two strips measuring 12 x 4cm (4¾ x 1½ in.)
- Coloured fusing glass: **Opalescent** 2mm (¹⁄₁₆ in.) thick, two pieces each in Gold Purple measuring 7 x 4cm (2¾ x 1½ in.), Neo Lavender 7 x 4cm (2¾ x 1½ in.), Cyan Blue 8 x 4cm (3 x 1½ in.), Vanilla 3.5 x 4cm (1⅜ x 1½ in.) and Deco Grey 4 x 6cm (1½ x 2⅜ in.); one piece each in Egyptian Blue measuring 14.5 x 1cm (5¾ x ⅜ in.), Marigold 14.5 x 1cm (5¾ x ⅜ in.), Pea Pod opalescent triangle 3cm (1¼ in.) each side and Tomato Red 3 x 1.5cm (1¼ x ⅝ in.)
- Stringers 1mm (¹⁄₃₂ in.) in Red
- Glass beads in various colours
- Glass glue
- Glassline pens in Orange Red, Yellow, Metallic Gold, Grey and Dark Blue
- 3mm (³⁄₃₂ in.) fibre paper
- Thinfire shelf paper
- Epoxy glue

EQUIPMENT

- Safety goggles
- Cutting surface
- Oil-filled glass cutter
- Grozing pliers
- Jewellery pliers
- Scribe
- Glue brush
- Fine black marker pen
- Paper towels
- Vinegar or glass cleaner
- Grinder
- Kiln

This is a project that is best constructed on a kiln shelf, or directly in the kiln, because it is made in pieces and may be hard to move once it is laid out. After the tack firing, the frame will require a second firing, a slump firing, to create an indentation in the back that the mirror glass can be glued into.

I've chosen a palette of blues with green and yellow accents as these colours look great in my bathroom, which is where my mirror will live. You should choose colours that work for your room décor, remembering that the glass needs to be opalescent.

1   Draw around the square of mirror glass onto a piece of paper.

2   Draw a 12 x 12cm (4¾ x 4¾ in.) square inside the first square and a 20 x 20cm (8 x 8 in.) square outside it. The frame will overlap the edge of the mirror by 1cm (⅜ in.) on all sides, giving a 12 x 12cm (4¾ x 4¾ in.) mirror in the finished piece.

3   Cut the strips of clear glass for the frame and fit onto the drawing. Place the two shorter pieces at the top and bottom and the longer pieces at the sides.

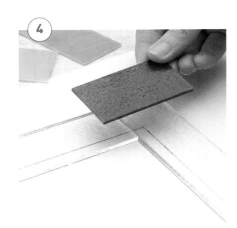

4 | Glue one piece of Neo Lavender opalescent glass to the top left-hand side so that it overlaps the join in the clear glass. Do the same with the second piece at the bottom right-hand side of the panel. Now glue the Gold Purple opalescent pieces to the top right-hand and bottom left-hand corners of the square. Take care not to move the clear pieces when gluing on the colours.

5 | Glue a Cyan Blue opalescent piece at the top and bottom of the panel, next to the Gold Purple pieces. Glue the pieces of Deco Grey opalescent between the Gold Purple and the Neo Lavender pieces. To complete the frame, add the squares of Vanilla opalescent.

6 | For decoration add the other smaller pieces of glass, following the photograph for position.

7 Now add the red stringers and the beads.

8 Finally add the finishing touches with the Glassline pens. Full or tack fuse fire the frame (see page 21).

9 Cut a piece of 3mm (³⁄₃₂ in.) fibre paper measuring 15 x 15cm (6 x 6 in.).

10 Make sure the fibre paper is square in the centre of the mirror frame. Place it back on the kiln shelf and fire at slump firing temperature (see page 21).

11 After you have removed the frame from the kiln, clean the back of it with vinegar or glass cleaner.

12 Following the manufacturer's instructions, apply some epoxy glue to the back of the frame.

13 Place the mirror glass onto the back of the frame and leave to dry.

SMALL
SQUARE MOON DISH

MATERIALS
- Clear fusing glass 3mm (³⁄₃₂ in.) thick measuring 10 x 10cm (4 x 4 in.)
- Coloured fusing glass in sheets: **Transparent** 2mm (¹⁄₁₆ in.) thick in Midnight Blue measuring 7 x 7cm (2¾ x 2¾ in.), four pieces in True Blue measuring 1.5 x 1.5cm (⅝ x ⅝ in.)
- Selection of small pieces of opalescent and transparent blue glass
- Dichroic glass Ripple Yellow/Blue on black
- Small pieces of dichroic glass offcuts
- Glass glue
- Thinfire shelf paper

EQUIPMENT
- Glass cutter
- Set square
- White marker pen
- Jewellery pliers
- Square slumping mould 11 x 11 x 1cm (4½ x 4½ x ⅜ in.)
- Template (see page 124)

This little dish can be used as a night-light holder or as a home for small pieces of jewellery. You could vary the design by using different colours for the border or by choosing some textured clear dichroic glass for the moon.

Make a complementary sun dish (see below) by cutting a circle of a Warm Yellow opalescent glass and gluing it onto a square of clear glass the same size as the moon dish. Add flame shapes cut from a variety of yellow and orange glass radiating out from the circle.

Finally add some scraps of dichroic glass, frits and pieces of rod to create texture in the centre of the sun and to add sparkle to the flames. Fire as for the moon dish.

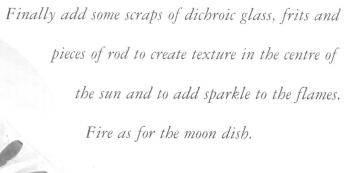

1 | Glue the Midnight Blue transparent glass in the centre of the clear square.

2 | Glue a square of True Blue transparent in each corner of the clear square.

3 | Cut small rectangles of blue glass to fit along the edge of the square and glue them in place.

4

5

6

4 Using the white pen and the template, trace the moon shape onto the back of the dichroic glass and cut it out. (This very textured glass can be quite hard to cut.)

5 Grind the moon to shape and glue it onto the dark blue square.

7

6 Using the dichroic offcuts, cut some tiny pieces to create the stars and glue them in place.

7 Fire the dish at full fuse temperature. Fire the fused square again on the mould at slump temperature (see page 21).

VIENNA
BOWL

MATERIALS
- Clear fusing glass 3mm (³⁄₃₂ in.) thick, circle measuring 23cm (9 in) diameter
- Coloured fusing glass in sheets:
  Transparent 2mm (¹⁄₁₆ in.) thick in Aquamarine, Deep Royal Blue, Emerald Green, Fuchsia, Light Green, Pine Green and True Blue
  Opalescent 2mm (¹⁄₁₆ in.) thick in Light Cyan Blue, Petal Pink, Spring Green, Sunflower Yellow, Tangerine Orange and White
- Dichroic glass in Soft Ripple Rainbow 2 on clear
- Frits (medium) in Sunflower Yellow
- Stringers 2mm (¹⁄₁₆ in.) in Sunflower Yellow
- Glass glue
- Thinfire shelf paper

EQUIPMENT
- Safety goggles
- Dust mask
- Cutting surface
- Oil-filled glass cutter
- Grozing pliers
- Jewellery pliers
- Set square
- Round slumping mould 23cm (9½ in.) diameter and 4cm (2 in.) deep with approx 4cm (2 in) rim
- Scribe
- Glue brush
- Fine black marker pen
- Paper towels
- Vinegar or glass cleaner
- Grinder
- Kiln

On a trip to Vienna a few years ago, I visited an exhibition by Gustav Klimt and was drawn to the fantastically rich colours and textures in his paintings. The circular patterns in this bowl are created by layering pieces of both transparent and opalescent glass together and then adding stringers and frits for extra texture.

This project takes a fairly long time to complete because there is quite a lot of cutting involved, but it is well worth the effort when you see the finished bowl. You will need to complete this project in two firings, the first being a full fuse firing followed by a slump firing over a circular mould.

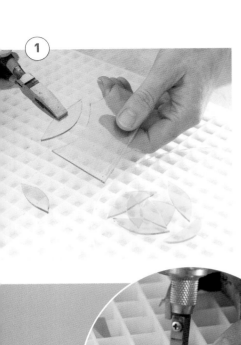

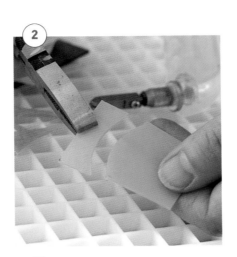

5

1   Cut sheets of glass into small squares then start to cut out circular pieces of glass. Draw the shape freehand onto the glass with the cutting tool. Do not worry if the circles are not perfect and if the sizes vary, as variations will make the design more interesting.

2   Refine the shapes by removing excess pieces of glass using the grozing pliers.

3   Use the grinder to grind off any rough edges, then clean and dry each glass disc.

4   Cut a circle of Soft Ripple Rainbow clear dichroic glass. This is a heavily textured glass that is easier to cut on the reverse. This piece will form an eye-catching centrepiece to the bowl.

5   To make triangles for the rim of the bowl, use a set square and glass cutter to cut a strip 2cm (¾ in.) wide from transparent Aquamarine glass.

6

6   Cut, then snip, triangles of glass and set them aside for use in Step 12. At the same time, make some smaller triangles from offcuts of coloured glass.

7   Arrange the first layer of coloured glass discs on the circular glass base. Once you are happy with the arrangement, apply a small amount of glass glue with a paintbrush to fix them in position. Make sure you leave plenty of room at the edge of the circle for the triangular rim design.

7

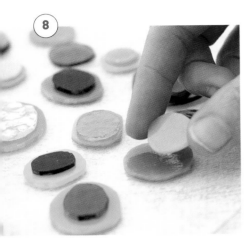

8 | When you have completed the first layer of circles, begin to add smaller circles on top of them. Glue these in position.

9 | Add the stringers. Brush a little glass glue in the places between the circles and measure the space where you want to place a piece of stringer.

10 | Break the stringer using the grozing pliers or snap them with your fingers. Push the pieces into position with a scribe.

11 | Brush a little glue in the spaces between the circles, then sprinkle on the frits. Use a fine, dry brush to remove any that have landed in the wrong place.

12 Start to arrange the triangles cut in Steps 5 and 6 around the rim of the dish, but do not glue them down until you have completed the circle. You may have to cut some slightly smaller to fit. Add coloured triangles elsewhere on the dish.

13 Cut a circle of Thinfire shelf paper to fit the kiln shelf, making sure there is at least 2.5cm (1 in.) of paper around the edge of the glass.

14 Place the finished glass circle on the paper and fire at full fuse temperature (see page 21). Once the firing is complete and the glass is cold, clean off the Thinfire paper with a wet paper towel or wet sponge.

15 Place the fired glass circle on top of the mould, put it back into the kiln and fire again at slump firing temperature (see page 21).

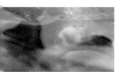

PERFORATED
PLATE

MATERIALS
- Pieces of clear glass
- Pieces of transparent and opalescent green glass
- Small pieces of clear and green on black dichroic glass
- Glass glue
- Thinfire shelf paper

EQUIPMENT
- Safety goggles
- Cutting surface
- Oil-filled glass cutter
- Grozing pliers
- Glue brush
- Paper towels
- Vinegar or glass cleaner
- Grinder
- Kiln shelf
- Round slumping mould 19cm (7½ in.) diameter and 3.5cm (1¼ in.) deep
- Kiln

I had so much scrap clear glass that I thought I would try to make a project from it; the result is this perforated plate. Simply leaving gaps between the pieces of glass when you put them together creates the holes. Do not forget to clean all the pieces of glass before starting.

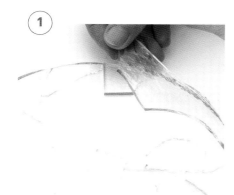

1 Draw a 18cm (7 in.) diameter circle onto the Thinfire paper on the kiln shelf. Arrange pieces of clear glass in the circle, overlapping the shapes, but making sure there are some gaps so that holes will form during firing.

2 Add some pieces of green glass.

3 Finally add some small scrap pieces of dichroic glass.

4 Fire at full fuse temperature (see page 21). Prepare the mould and fire again on a slump cycle (see page 21).

SMALL
ROUND FLOWER DISH

MATERIALS

- Clear fusing glass 3mm (³⁄₃₂ in.) thick, circle measuring 19cm (7.5 in.) diameter
- Coloured fusing glass in sheets:
  Transparent 2mm (¹⁄₁₆ in.) thick in Marigold Yellow, Olive Green, Cranberry, Emerald Green and small pieces of various shades of green
  Opalescent 2mm (¹⁄₁₆ in.) thick in Light Cyan Blue, Sunflower Yellow, Peach Cream and small pieces in shades of green
- Stringers 2mm (¹⁄₁₆ in.) in Sunflower Yellow opalescent and 1mm (¹⁄₃₂ in.) in Pink
- Frits (medium) in Marigold Yellow transparent, Sunflower Yellow transparent, Pumpkin Orange opalescent, Tangerine Orange opalescent, Pink opalescent, Teal Green opalescent, Spring Green opalescent and Tangerine Orange opalescent
- Rods in Red and Yellow
- Glass glue
- Thinfire shelf paper

This little dish contains a posy of flowers surrounded by a circle of green leaves. Displayed with sunlight streaming through it, the flowers really come to life. The shallow shape also works well if you want to make a variation of the Vienna Bowl (see page 76) with coloured glass circles (see below).

EQUIPMENT

- Safety goggles
- Cutting surface
- Oil-filled glass cutter
- Grozing pliers
- Jewellery pliers
- Scribe
- Glue brush
- Fine black marker pen
- Paper towels
- Vinegar or glass cleaner
- Grinder
- Kiln
- Round slumping mould 19cm (7½ in) diameter and 3.5cm (1¼ in.) deep
- Template (see page 124)

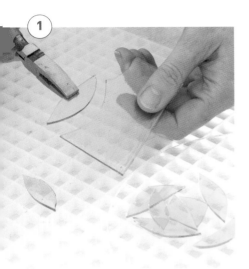

1 Cut petal shapes out of Marigold Yellow transparent glass.

2 Form a rose shape by overlapping the pieces, gluing them in place as you go. Don't put the flower too close to the edge of the clear circle; you need to leave enough space for the border.

3 Brush a little glue in the centre of the rose and sprinkle on some Marigold Yellow transparent and Pumpkin Orange opalescent frits. Cut out some leaves from Olive

Green transparent glass and glue them next to the rose.

4 Using the petal template, cut out five petals from Light Cyan Blue opalescent.

5 Glue the petals into a flower shape with the points touching. Using a small lid as a template, cut out a circle of Sunflower Yellow opalescent.

6 Glue the circle into the centre of the blue flower. Add some pieces of Sunflower Yellow opalescent stringer, radiating out from the centre.

7 Sprinkle a few Tangerine Orange opalescent frits onto the blue flower.

8 Create the border by cutting some leaf shapes out of the small pieces of different types of green glass. Arrange the leaves around the edge of the clear circle, leaving a space about 1cm (⅜ in.) wide between each.

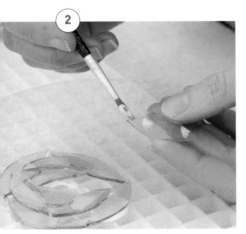

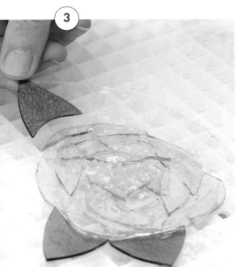

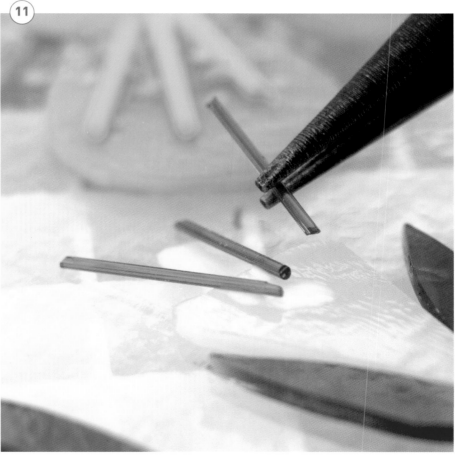

9 Add a small pile of Tangerine Orange opalescent frits in the space between each leaf.

10 For the fuchsias, cut two triangles of Peach Cream opalescent and grind off the corners. Glue them in place then add two petals of Cranberry transparent to each flower.

11 Add some pink stringers and frits for the stamens and long pieces of Emerald Green transparent for stems. In the space remaining on the clear glass, make a daisy out of Sunflower Yellow opalescent petals with a piece of red rod in the centre.

12 | Finally, add some background texture using Teal Green opalescent, Marigold Yellow transparent and Spring Green opalescent frits. Fire at full fuse temperature (see page 21).

13 | Place the fused circle on top of the mould and fire again at slump firing temperature (see page 21).

CURVED
ARC PANEL

MATERIALS
- Clear fusing glass 3mm (³⁄₃₂ in.) thick measuring 15 x 33.5cm (6 x 13¼ in.)
- Coloured fusing glass in sheets:
  Transparent 2mm (¹⁄₁₆ in.) thick in Yellow measuring 18 x 4cm (7 x 1½ in.), Yellow measuring 20 x 3cm (8 x 1¼ in.), Light Coral Striker measuring 10.5 x 2cm (4⅛ x ¾ in.), Aquamarine Blue four pieces each measuring 10 x 0.5cm (4 x ¼ in.), Chartreuse Green four pieces each measuring 10 x 0.5cm (4 x ¼ in.), Light Aquamarine measuring 2.5 x 2.5cm (1 x 1 in.), Coral Striker measuring 2.5 x 2.5cm (1 x 1 in.), strips of Light Plum measuring 1cm (⅜ in.) wide and three Tan triangles measuring 2.5cm (1 in.) each side
  Opalescent 2mm (¹⁄₁₆ in.) thick in Cobalt Blue, five wavy strips measuring approx 15cm (6 in.) long and three Aquamarine triangles measuring 2.5cm (1 in.) each side
- Ten 2mm (¹⁄₁₆ in.) strips of opalescent and transparent glass measuring approx 4 x 0.8cm (1½ x ⅜ in.)
- 2mm (¹⁄₁₆ in.) transparent and opalescent glass circles, eight measuring 3cm (1¼ in.) in diameter and eight 2cm (¾ in.) in diameter
- Small pieces of dichroic glass
- Stringers 2mm (¹⁄₁₆ in.) in Sunflower Yellow
- Confetti in Cobalt Blue opalescent
- Pieces of White rod
- Frits (medium) in Lemon Yellow and Turquoise Blue opalescent
- Glassline pens in Gold, Yellow, and Lavender
- Glass glue
- Thinfire shelf paper

EQUIPMENT
- Safety goggles
- Cutting surface
- Oil-filled glass cutter
- Grozing pliers
- Jewellery pliers
- Scribe
- Glue brush
- Dry paintbrush
- Cutting square
- Fine black marker pen
- Paper towels
- Vinegar or glass cleaner
- Grinder
- Kiln
- Arc mould (or lamp bender) 22 x 26.5 x 9.5cm (8¾ x 10½ x 3¾ in.)

Arcs are curved, free-standing panels that look great on a windowsill with natural light coming through them, or on a table with a candle behind. They can be fully fused before being slumped or, like the version shown opposite, tack fused. You can also make double arcs that are a gentle 'S' shape, like the beach scene double arc, below.

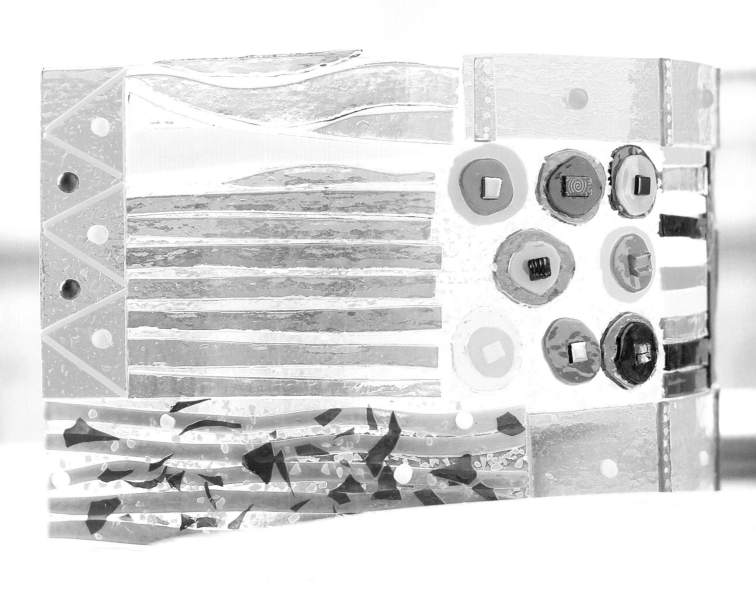

1 | Arrange the pieces of Cobalt Blue opalescent on the bottom left-hand side of the clear panel. Add the 4cm (1½ in.) wide strip of Yellow transparent glass to the bottom right-hand area of the panel and the longer strip of Yellow transparent glass along the top right-hand edge of the panel.

Add the strip of Coral Striker to the top left-hand side, at right-angles to the pieces of Cobalt Blue opalescent. Above the Cobalt Blue opalescent strips, add alternate pieces of Aquamarine transparent and Chartreuse transparent. Above these, add some long triangular pieces of opalescent and transparent glass.

Place alternate squares of Light Aqua transparent and Coral transparent on the right-hand side of the panel between the Yellow transparent pieces. To the left of the squares, add the triangles of Aquamarine opalescent and Tan transparent (you will have to cut one of the triangles in half to make it fit).

Add the ten 4 x 0.8cm (1½ x ⅜ in.) strips of glass in a vertical row next to the triangles. Now add the large circles of glass to the centre of the panel and put the smaller pieces on top. Add some strips of Light Plum to break up the yellow panels; add three at the top and two longer ones at the bottom.

2 | Add some broken pieces of Cobalt Blue opalescent confetti to the Cobalt Blue strips. Decorate them further with pieces of White rod and some Lemon Yellow frits.

3 | Decorate the Coral Striker piece of glass (which appears clear and colourless until fired) with some pieces of Lemon Yellow stringer arranged in triangles. Add some beads to the centre of each triangle and also to the centre of each Yellow rectangle.

4 | Finally place some Turquoise opalescent frits between the circles and brush away any that land in the wrong place. Using the Glassline pens, add some Gold and Yellow spirals onto the Light Aqua and Coral squares and some dots to the triangles and to the Light Plum strips. When the Glassline decorations have dried, fire the panel at full fuse firing (see page 21).

5 | Slump fuse the panel over a prepared arc mould (see page 21).

6 | Before closing the kiln, check that the bottom edge of the panel is parallel to the edge of the mould otherwise, once the panel is fired it will not stand up straight.

3

5

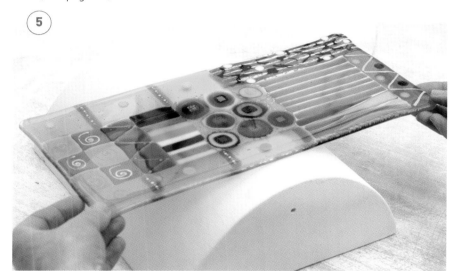

4

6

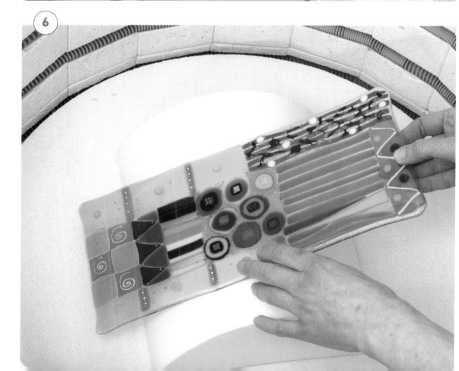

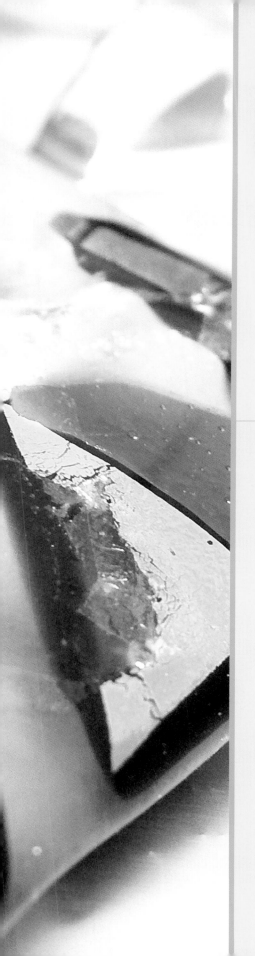

JEWELLERY
AND DECORATIONS

THE RICH, SHIMMERING QUALITIES OF COLOURED GLASS
MAKE IT IDEAL FOR CREATING STUNNING JEWELLERY. AS THE
PIECES IN THIS CHAPTER ARE ALL ON SUCH A SMALL SCALE,
THEY ARE QUICK AND FUN TO MAKE.

ZIGZAG
MAGNET

MATERIALS
- Clear fusing glass 2mm (⅟₁₆ in.) thick
- Opalescent 2mm (⅟₁₆ in.) thick in Pea Pod Green
- Stringers in a range of colours
- Glass glue
- Thinfire shelf paper
- Epoxy glue
- Magnet

EQUIPMENT
- Safety goggles
- Cutting surface
- Oil-filled glass cutter
- Grozing pliers
- Jewellery pliers
- Scribe
- Tea light or small candle
- Matches
- Glue brush
- Fine black marker pen
- Paper towels
- Vinegar or glass cleaner
- Grinder
- Kiln

Stringers bend quite easily when held over a candle flame and so it's easy to create zigzags with them. You will notice a sooty residue on the stringer after it has been in the flame, but this can easily be wiped off once the glass has cooled.

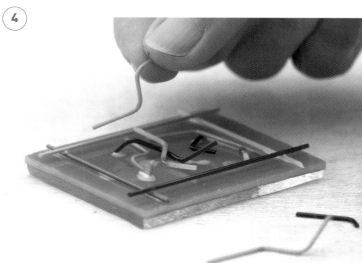

1 | Cut a rectangle of clear glass and a rectangle of Pea Pod Green glass the same size.

2 | Break a stringer to the length of each side of the rectangle and glue them in place.

3 | To bend a stringer, hold it over a tea light flame until the stringer bends in the heat. Turn the stringer over and bend it again further along its length to create a zigzag.

4 | Leave the zigzags to cool, wipe clean then glue them onto the green glass. Fire at full fuse temperature (see page 21). When completed, glue the magnet onto the back of the glass using epoxy glue.

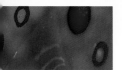

BIG FISH
LITTLE FISH

MATERIALS
- Clear fusing glass 2mm (1/16 in.) thick measuring approx 18 x 10cm (7 x 4 in.)
- Coloured fusing glass in sheets: **Opalescent** 2mm (1/16 in.) thick in Steel Blue, Tomato Red and Cobalt Blue
- Small pieces of dichroic glass
- Stringers 1mm (1/32 in.) in Cobalt Blue
- Beads or pieces of rod
- Glass glue
- 20-gauge and 18-gauge copper wire
- Glassline pens in Red and Yellow
- Thinfire shelf paper
- Ribbon for hanging

EQUIPMENT
- Safety goggles
- Cutting surface
- Oil-filled glass cutter
- Grozing pliers
- Jewellery pliers
- Scribe
- Glue brush
- Fine black marker pen
- Wire cutters
- Paper towels
- Vinegar or glass cleaner
- Grinder
- Kiln
- Templates (see page 126)

I am often asked to make pieces to display in bathrooms and fish are a frequently requested theme. You can have a lot of fun with colour and patterns and can make them as exotic-looking as you wish, and they are lovely made from glass because the sheen makes them look permanently wet. You can make smaller individual fish (see page 101), or try making this Big Fish, Little Fish decoration.

This project is one that is best not moved too much once it is assembled, so either make it directly in the kiln or on a lined kiln shelf. The tricky part is fitting the wire connecting the two fish, but as long as you double check it is in the right place before you close the kiln, all should be well. I usually use opalescent glass because the density of the colour disguises the ends of the copper wire hangers.

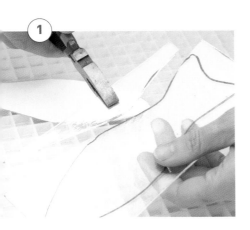

1 Draw round the big fish template onto clear glass. Starting from the tail end of the fish, make a cut to about half way down the body of the fish then go off at the edge. Break off this section of glass. Cut down the rest of the side to the nose end. Finish cutting out the fish shape in the same way. Using the little fish template, trace and cut out a little fish. Grind off any rough edges.

2 Lay the clear glass big fish on the Steel Blue opalescent so that you can trace the fish body without the tail and the nose. Cut out the body shape. Lay the clear glass little fish on the Steel Blue and trace then cut out the whole body.

3 Trace the nose and tail of the big fish onto the Tomato Red opalescent and cut them out. Check that all the shapes fit together neatly.

4 From the 20-gauge wire, cut and bend into shape two hooks. Glue them to the top edge of the clear glass big fish, one just behind the head and the other on the tail. Cut a 6cm (2⅜ in.) length of the 18-gauge wire and glue one end

to the middle of the lower edge of the big fish and one to the tip of the nose of the little fish. Glue the coloured body of the little fish onto the clear glass, over the wire. Glue on the body, nose and tail of the big fish.

5 For the fins, cut a triangle of Cobalt Blue opalescent and glue one onto the body of each fish. Cut small pieces of dichroic glass

for the eyes, grind off the edges and glue in place. Add three pieces of stringer to each tail.

6 Finish off by decorating the fish using beads or pieces of glass rod. Add red circles with yellow dots using the Glassline pens. Fire at tack or full fuse firing (see page 21). Add ribbon to hang up your fish.

CAT FRIDGE MAGNET

MATERIALS
- Clear fusing glass 2mm (⅟₁₆ in.) thick measuring approx 6 x 6cm (2½ x 2 in.)
- Piece of yellow Glassline paper
- Glassline pens in Gold, Dark Blue and White
- Glass glue
- Thinfire shelf paper
- Epoxy glue
- Magnet

EQUIPMENT
- Safety goggles
- Cutting surface
- Oil-filled glass cutter
- Grozing pliers
- Jewellery pliers
- Scissors
- Ruler
- Template (see page 126)
- Fine black marker pen
- Paper towels
- Vinegar or glass cleaner
- Grinder
- Kiln

Glassline paper is made especially for fusing: it can be drawn on, cut with scissors or torn. It should be fired between two layers of glass and you will need to leave a border of glass around the edge of the paper to make sure the glass pieces fuse together properly.

1. Draw around the template onto clear glass and cut out the shape, then grind it if necessary. Using the white marker pen to draw with, do the same with the Black glass.

2. Grind the Black glass into shape.

3. Cut a thin strip of gold leaf and lay it across the centre of the pendant. Gold leaf is very fine and tears easily so handle it carefully.

4. Using the white pen, draw round the top half of the template onto the Aurora Borealis Cool dichroic glass. Cut out and grind the shape if needed.

5. Put a little glue onto the top part of the Black base and glue on the clear glass. Then glue on the dichroic glass.

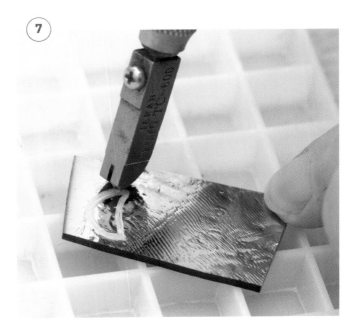

6 Draw around the bottom part of the template onto the Savoy Sandart dichroic glass and cut out. Check that it fits the bottom part of the pendant and grind if necessary, then glue in place with a small amount of glue.

7 Draw a very small crescent moon onto a piece of dichroic glass and cut out then grind it to get the shape right.

8 Glue on the moon then when all of the glue is dry, carefully cut off any extra gold leaf with a sharp knife. Fire at full fuse temperature (see page 21).

VASE
OF FLOWERS BROOCH

MATERIALS
- Clear fusing glass 2mm (1/16 in.) or 3mm (3/32 in.) thick
- Aventurine Green glass
- Triangle of Yellow opalescent glass
- Small pieces of White, Yellow and Red rods
- Stringers 1mm (1/32 in.) in Orange
- Glassline pens in Red, Orange and Yellow
- Thinfire shelf paper
- Large brooch back
- Glass glue
- Epoxy glue

EQUIPMENT
- Safety goggles
- Cutting surface
- Oil-filled glass cutter
- Grozing pliers
- Jewellery pliers
- Scribe
- Ruler
- Fine black marker pen
- Glue brush
- Paper towels
- Vinegar or glass cleaner
- Grinder
- Kiln

This brooch is quite chunky but would look good on a coat or heavy sweater. The Aventurine Green glass has a lovely sparkle to it.

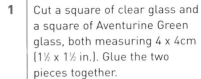

1 Cut a square of clear glass and a square of Aventurine Green glass, both measuring 4 x 4cm (1½ x 1½ in.). Glue the two pieces together.

2 Cut a small triangle of Yellow opalescent glass and place on the lower edge of the Green glass. Add five pieces of Orange stringer.

3 Cut some pieces of Red, Yellow and White rods.

4 Glue a piece of rod at the end of each piece of stringer.

5 Draw a pattern around the edge of the green square using the Yellow Glassline pen. With the Red Glassline pen, add some dots and a stripe on the yellow triangle. Finally add a small piece of dichroic glass on the red stripe. Fire at either tack fuse or full fuse temperature (see page 21).

6 After the piece is fired, glue a large brooch back onto the glass.

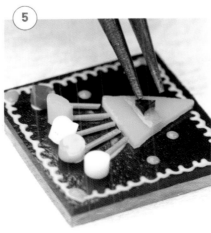

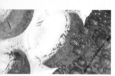

BUBBLE

PENDANT

Bubble Effect powder is fun to use and this simple pendant is easy to make. You could try experimenting with different-coloured Bubble Effect powders.

MATERIALS
- Clear fusing glass 2mm (⅟₁₆ in.) thick measuring 2 x 6cm (¾ x 2⅜ in.)
- Dichroic glass Violet on thin Black
- Dichroic glass Radium/Ripple Rainbow on clear
- Blue Bubble Effect powder
- Thinfire shelf paper
- Sterling silver tube-top bail
- Glass glue
- Epoxy glue

EQUIPMENT
- Safety goggles
- Cutting surface
- Oil-filled glass cutter
- Grozing pliers
- Ruler
- Dry brush
- Paper towels
- Vinegar or glass cleaner
- Kiln

1   With a dry brush, apply a little Bubble Effect powder to the clear base glass. Take care not to apply too much, as this will create large bubbles. Put a dab of glue on each corner and put the second piece of clear glass on top.

2   Cut a piece of the Violet dichroic glass for the top of the pendant and check that it is long enough to cover the silver bail when that is glued onto the back. Cut another smaller piece for the bottom of the pendant then glue both pieces in place.

3   Cut a strip of the clear dichroic glass and glue it on down the centre of the pendant, between the two pieces of Violet dichroic glass. Fire at tack fuse or full fuse temperature (see page 21). After firing, use epoxy glue to fix the bail onto the back of the pendant.

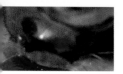

GLASS
PENDANT

MATERIALS
- Scraps of glass
- Glass glue
- Thinfire shelf paper
- Jump ring

EQUIPMENT
- Safety goggles
- Oil-filled glass cutter
- Grozing pliers
- Jewellery pliers
- Scribe
- Glue brush
- Thinfire paper
- Kiln

Working with glass you always end up with a lot of small scrap pieces and this pendant is a way of using them up. You can be as inventive as you like about how you make these pendants!

①

②

1 Arrange the pieces of glass directly onto a kiln shelf lined with Thinfire paper, placing them so that there is a gap at the top of the arrangement for the jump ring. You could use a piece of fibre paper or fibre rope to keep the hole open. Fire at tack fuse or full fuse temperature (see page 21).

2 Attach a jump ring through the hole at the top.

114

CHRISTMAS
DECORATIONS

STOCKING MATERIALS
- Clear fusing glass 2mm (¹⁄₁₆ in.) thick measuring approx 10 x 8cm (4 x 3 in.)
- Coloured fusing glass in sheets:
  Transparent 2mm (¹⁄₁₆ in.) thick in Kelly Green
  Opalescent 2mm (¹⁄₁₆ in.) thick in Tomato Red, White Streaky, Spring Green, Jade Green and small triangles of Orange
- Glassline pens in Gold and Red Orange
- Stringers 1mm (¹⁄₃₂ in.) in Red
- 20-gauge copper wire
- Glass glue
- Thinfire shelf paper
- Ribbon for hanging

EQUIPMENT
- Safety goggles
- Cutting surface
- Oil-filled glass cutter
- Grozing pliers
- Jewellery pliers
- Scribe
- Glue brush
- Fine black marker pen
- Wire cutters
- Grinder
- Kiln
- Template (see page 126)

Made from small pieces of colourful glass, these hanging Christmas decorations will look great on your tree or elsewhere in the house. They are also perfect holiday gifts, so make batches of each type and give them to friends to celebrate the season. Choose suitably festive colours or experiment with bold colours for a contemporary style.

You could try making larger versions of the stockings by enlarging the template on a photocopier. However, be aware that if they are larger they will also be heavier and you may choose to hang them on a wall rather than on your Christmas tree!

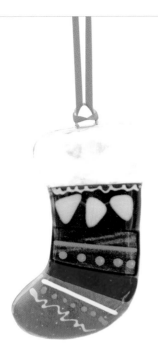

STOCKING

This little stocking is light enough to hang on your Christmas tree, or you could make several and attach them to a long string or ribbon to decorate a window.

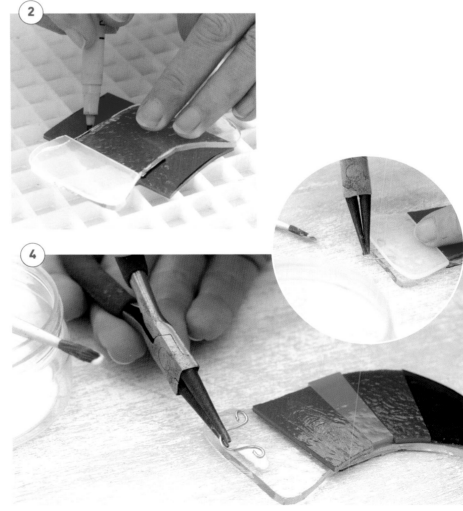

1 Using the template, draw the stocking shape onto 2mm (⅟₁₆ in.) clear glass. Cut out the shape, taking care when cutting the curves. Cut a piece of the White Streaky opalescent for the top of the stocking (you can draw the top of the stocking shape onto the glass using a marker pen).

2 Using the clear stocking as a guide, cut out the top of the stocking from White Streaky. Cut stripes of Tomato Red opalescent and the green opalescents until the rest of the stocking base is covered in coloured stripes.

3 Cut a piece of 20-gauge wire approx 5cm (2 in.) long and bend it into a hook.

4 Glue the wire at the top of the stocking and lay the White Streaky piece over the top.

5 Now glue all the coloured stripes in place on the base.

6 Add some small triangles of Orange opalescent and some pieces of Red stringer.

7 Using the Gold and Red Orange Glassline pens, decorate the stocking with zigzags and dots. Fire in the kiln at tack fuse temperature (see page 21).

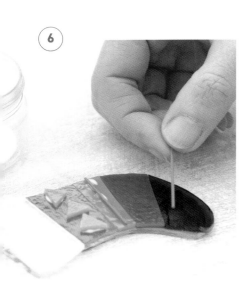

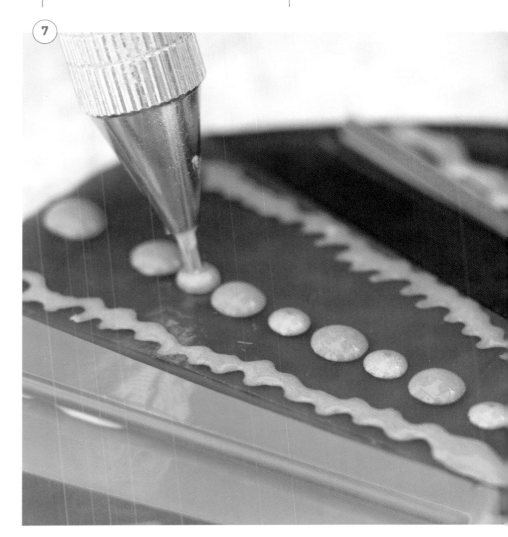

CHRISTMAS TREE

There are lots of different shades of green so you could choose a different colour for this tree. The Aventurine Green used to make the Vase of Flowers Brooch (see page 110) would be a particularly good choice because it has a sparkle to it.

MATERIALS

- Clear fusing glass 2mm (1/16 in.) thick measuring approx 11.5 x 6cm (4½ x 2½ in.)
- Coloured fusing glass in sheets: **Opalescent** 2mm (1/16 in.) thick in Pea Pod and Tomato Red
- Small pieces of dichroic glass
- Stringers 1mm (1/32 in.) in Red
- 20-gauge copper wire
- Ribbon for hanging
- Glass glue
- Beads or pieces of rod
- Glassline pen in Gold
- Thinfire shelf paper

EQUIPMENT

- Safety goggles
- Cutting surface
- Oil-filled glass cutter
- Grozing pliers
- Jewellery pliers
- Wire cutter
- Glue brush
- Fine black marker pen
- Paper towels
- Vinegar or glass cleaner
- Grinder
- Kiln
- Templates (see page 126)

1 | Using the tree template, trace and cut the shape in clear glass. Do the same with the pot. Repeat using the Pea Pod for the tree and Tomato Red for the pot.

2 | Check that the coloured glass pieces are the same size as the base pieces.

3 | Cut a piece of copper wire approx 4cm (1½ in.) long and bend it into a hook. Glue it to the clear glass at the top of the Christmas tree.

4 | Glue the Pea Pod glass on top of base and add some Red stringers for decoration. Take a small square of dichroic glass and grind off the corners to make a circle. Glue this on at the top of the tree.

5 | Now glue on the Tomato Red pot and add a strip of dichroic glass for decoration. Add some beads to the tree and finally decorate it with the Gold Glassline pen. When placing the tree in the kiln, make sure that the tree and the pot are touching so that during firing they will fuse together. Fire at tack fusing temperature (see page 21)

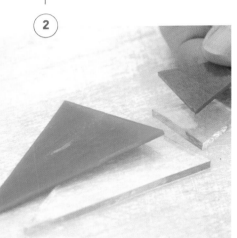

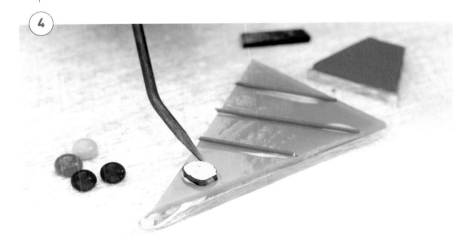

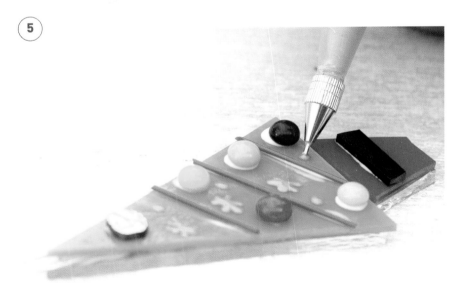

SMALL STAR

These stars are lovely to make as Christmas presents, but could be appropriate for any time of the year. They look particularly effective made in different sizes and hung in a window. The stars will need to be constructed in the kiln or on a kiln shelf.

1 | Using the template, trace and cut out six triangles in clear glass. Place them on the lined kiln shelf with all the points touching. Make sure the gaps between each triangle are equal.

2 | Using the same template, trace and cut out three Tomato Red triangles and three Marigold Yellow ones.

3 | Lay a red glass triangle on alternate clear ones.

①

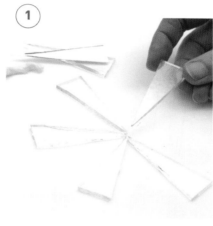

②

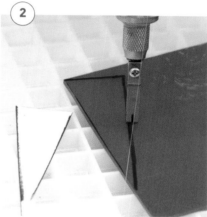

③

MATERIALS
- Clear fusing glass 3mm (³⁄₃₂ in.) thick, six pieces measuring approx 8 x 4cm (3 x 1½ in.)
- Coloured fusing glass in sheets: **Opalescent** 2mm (¹⁄₁₆ in.) thick in Tomato Red and Marigold Yellow
- Dichroic Dot 2 on thin clear glass
- Clear dichroic stringers
- Small triangles of dichroic glass, three on clear and three on black
- Copper sheet
- 3mm (³⁄₃₂ in.) fibre rope
- Thinfire shelf paper
- Ribbon

EQUIPMENT
- Safety goggles
- Cutting surface
- Oil-filled glass cutter
- Grozing pliers
- Jewellery pliers
- Scissors
- Scribe
- Heart-shaped punch
- Fine black marker pen
- Paper towels
- Vinegar or glass cleaner
- Grinder
- Kiln
- Template (see page 126)

4 Cut a piece of fibre rope 5cm (2 in.) long and lay it across the top of one of the clear triangles, about 2cm (¾ in.) down from the edge. The fibre rope will create a hole through which you can thread a ribbon. Place a triangle of the Marigold Yellow glass on top of the fibre rope; do not glue the fibre rope down, but you can use a bit of glue to hold the other triangles together.

5 Cut a circle of clear glass approx 4cm (1½ in.) in diameter and glue it into the centre of the star. Punch a heart out of the copper sheet and place in the centre of the clear circle, so that it is in line with the yellow triangle the fibre paper runs under.

6 Cut another circle from dichroic glass the same size as the clear glass circle and place this on top of the heart. Remember to remove the pen marks first.

7 Break some pieces of clear dichroic stringer and glue one onto each triangle, leaving a gap of about 2cm (¾ in.) at the top for the dichroic triangles.

8 Add small triangles of dichroic glass to the ends of the coloured triangles. Fire at tack fuse firing (see page 21). After firing, remove the fibre rope and wash the star in water with a little detergent. Add a ribbon to hang the star.

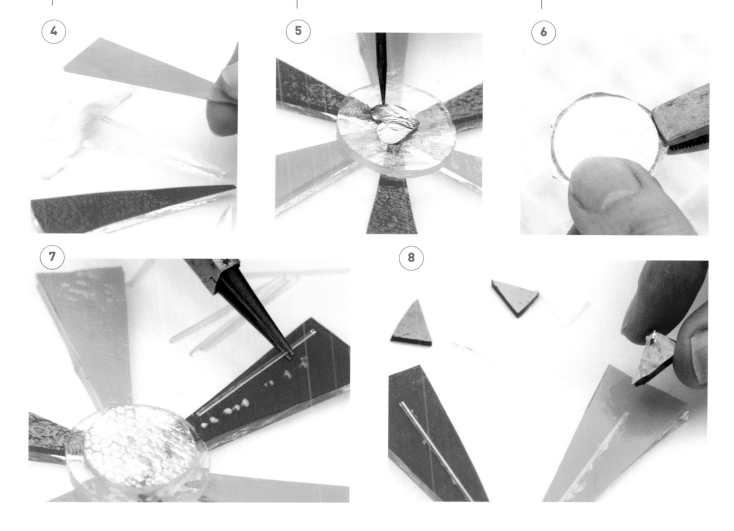

TEMPLATES

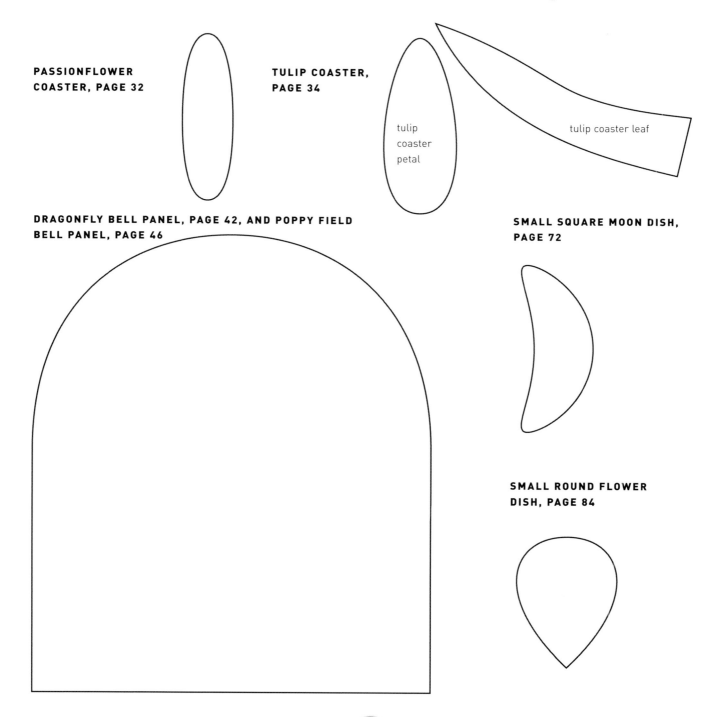

PASSIONFLOWER COASTER, PAGE 32

TULIP COASTER, PAGE 34

tulip coaster petal

tulip coaster leaf

DRAGONFLY BELL PANEL, PAGE 42, AND POPPY FIELD BELL PANEL, PAGE 46

SMALL SQUARE MOON DISH, PAGE 72

SMALL ROUND FLOWER DISH, PAGE 84